The Theory of the Firm

By the same author

INFLATION
MANAGERIAL ECONOMICS
ECONOMIC POLICY (with A. H. Fowler)

The Theory of the Firm

P. J. CURWEN

M

First edition 1976
Reprinted 1978,1979

Published by
THE MACMILLAN PRESS LTD
London and Basingstoke
Associated companies in Delhi Dublin
Hong Kong Johannesburg Lagos Melbourne
New York Singapore and Tokyo

ISBN 0 333 18847 0

Printed in Hong Kong

To Frank Neal and David Holmes

Contents

Introduction

Aims

This book is directed towards intermediate-level students taking either full-time or part-time degree and sub-degree-level courses in economics, business studies and management. It is directed particularly towards students on courses which concentrate more or less exclusively upon the subject-matter of that collection of economic models known generically as 'the theory of the firm', but it should also prove useful as a supplementary text for courses in microeconomic theory. It is assumed throughout the book that the reader is thoroughly acquainted with basic economic concepts.*

This book differs from others in the field in that it combines comprehensiveness of coverage with a relatively non-technical level of exposition and with a considerable emphasis upon empirical studies of the behaviour of firms. One complaint frequently voiced by students asked to plough their way through a multitude of alternative, and often conflicting, economic models, is that they have no effective means at their disposal of assessing the relative value of such models as descriptions of actual business behaviour. This book sets out to assist the student, so far as is possible, with this task by presenting whatever relevant empirical evidence is available, especially that which applies to the U.K. economy.

I have attempted to approach the various models of the firm which are examined in this book in a uniform way. I begin by detailing each model in its original formulation and follow this with an exposition of any extensions of the basic model as are of interest, a matter in

* Should, however, the reader wish to be reminded of such concepts before reading this book he is recommended to consult P. J. Curwen, *Managerial Economics* (London: Macmillan, 1974) ch. 1.

which I have had, of necessity, to exercise my personal judgement in order to keep the book as compact as possible. I subsequently detail valid criticisms of both the basic and extended formulations of the model, and finish up with an examination of any empirical studies which purport either to verify or disprove the ability of each model to predict behaviour in the real world.

This book is not, therefore, intended merely as an exercise in model building with the various models compared according to their respective responses to varying stimuli such as a change in the tax laws. Inevitably, however, the development of economic thought on the theory of the firm is best tackled through the sequential analysis of models of the firm. To this end the book begins with a survey of what is most commonly known as the 'traditional' theory of the firm. This I have taken to comprise the models of perfect competition, monopoly and monopolistic competition, the latter model being included here as a matter of convenience on the grounds that it is deeply rooted in the other models which preceded it. The basic variants of these models are probably familiar to anyone who has previously studied microeconomics. Nevertheless, it is important to explore them fully in the context of this book if only in order to appreciate why dissatisfaction with their assumptions sparked off the vast post-war literature on the theory of the firm.

The middle section of the book comprises an analysis of oligopoly. In this section we will be examining a cross-section of the best-known models of duopoly and oligopoly all of which incorporate the assumption of profit-maximising behaviour. In addition we will be outlining the precepts of the theory of games and questioning whether it has added anything to our stock of knowledge about the behaviour of firms. Another important area for study is the role of entry in the theory of the firm. This is important because, whereas entry is wholly unimpeded in perfect competition, it cannot take place under monopoly conditions. Hence the existence of entry restrictions which are empirically verifiable introduces the possibility of a whole range of complex interdependence situations between firms.

The final section of the book, which is approximately as long as the other two sections combined, is concerned with 'modern' or 'alternative' theories of the firm. The background to this section is provided by an examination of the assumptions, other than that about a firm's objectives, which underlie traditional models of the firm. Consideration is given to the nature of cost curves in order to discover what effect a non-U-shaped average-cost curve might have upon a firm's operating decisions. Also the process of price determination is fully explored in order to pave the way for the subsequent discussion of non-profit-maximising objectives. Finally, the problem of decision-making under conditions of uncertainty is analysed, with the same end in view.

The rest of the final section largely comprises a review of those models of the firm whose assumptions differ more or less completely from those of traditional models. These models are linked in particular by the manner in which the objective of profit maximisation is made subservient to alternative objective functions. It is important to have in mind, however, that the dropping of the objective of profit maximisation necessarily implies acceptance of the hypothesis that control of a corporate enterprise is vested in individuals other than those who own it. Many commentators are inclined to treat the separation of ownership from control as too obvious to warrant detailed examination. That this issue is far from cut and dried is, however, demonstrated by the review of the literature set out in the course of this particular section.

The book concludes with a review of the 'behavioural' theory of the firm which takes us out of the realm of pure economics and which introduces many concepts more familiar to students of the other social sciences. This is the most eclectic of the theories discussed in the course of the book and serves the useful purpose of pulling together much of what has gone before.

I have set out to avoid wherever possible the use of reference material for imparting information supplementary to that contained in the text itself as I feel that it is desirable to avoid frequent interruptions to the flow of the argument. There are, however, extensive references to source material which are to be found in the Notes at the end of the book (the Bibliography giving, where appropriate, the full data). I feel that, in a book which seeks to distil the ideas of a wide range of commentators, both teacher and student should be advised as to where they may find a more detailed exposition of ideas summarised in the book.

Methodology

One of the main purposes of this book is to examine the wide range of traditional and modern models * of the firm in order to discover whether any of them can justly claim to be *the* theory of the firm. In other words, we seek a theory which is sufficiently general to explain the behaviour of all firms within the economy, irrespective, for example, either of their size or of the degree of competition which they face.

The search for such a general theory of the firm is important for our understanding of the real world in many ways, by no means the least of which is the fact that an understanding of the behaviour of firms is essential if the government is to have effective control over the economy. It is manifestly obvious that the success of economic policy rests heavily upon the ability of the authorities to predict accurately what will happen when various measures are introduced, whether it be the effects upon wages, prices, investment, profits, or any other variable over which the typical firm has some form of control.

There are, however, considerable limitations upon our ability to construct a truly general theory of the firm, even if we restrict ourselves to what is commonly known as a capitalist economy. The most obvious difficulty is that we must put aside any consideration of firms which belong to the public sector of the economy, in particular the nationalised industries, even though these constitute a significant part of total productive capacity. This is because the objectives of such firms are heavily influenced by factors such as the 'public interest' which are, for the most part, incompatible with the objectives of firms in the private sector.

On a narrower, more technical level, we are faced with the inherent difficulties of model building. Typically the construction of a model goes through a number of stages, commencing with the identification of those variables whose inclusion in the theory is essential if it is to reflect at all accurately the real world. In practice, however, the workings of even a small firm are extremely complex, and we cannot hope to take into consideration every variable which has some implication, however small, for the realism of the model. It is therefore necessary

* The reader should be aware that the terms 'model' and 'theory' are used interchangeably in the course of this book.

to exclude all those variables whose existence does not materially affect the predictive ability of the theory, and it goes without saying that this is a complex task.

Once the essential variables have been isolated they are combined to form a model by assuming that they are interrelated in specific ways. Such interrelationships can be variously expressed, most commonly by verbal, geometrical, arithmetical, or algebraic formulations, although use is increasingly being made of econometric methods. Each variable can then be assigned a particular value and the model can be solved. By altering these variables a model can be manipulated to yield a set of predictions about how a firm will behave when subjected to varying stimuli, such as a change in taxation or overheads. The validity of the model then depends upon whether or not the predictions which it throws up reflect the real-life operations of firms. If we find that a firm actually does react to a change in taxation in the manner prescribed by the model then the model is adjudged acceptable. If, however, the predictions do not accord with reality the model builder must alter his model in some way in order to produce predictions more in accord with reality, and this process must, if necessary, be continually repeated until a decision is eventually taken either to accept or reject the model.

It is sometimes argued that a model should only be accepted if its assumptions are realistic. This requirement is, however, very difficult to satisfy simply because the process of abstracting the essential variables for a model often necessitates the use of concepts which are little used by practising managers. For the purposes of this book we are therefore proceeding on the basis that the validity of the models discussed therein depends upon the accuracy of their predictions. On this basis we will be examining such empirical evidence as is available for the purposes of testing the predictive ability of each separate model.

Finally we may note that, whereas it is a simple matter to disprove a theory simply by providing one instance in which it fails to conform with reality, a theory cannot be proven true simply by providing one instance in which it does accord with reality. Indeed, in so far as it is impossible to test empirically every possible prediction which a model could conceivably produce through altering its components either singly or in combination, a theory can only be treated as acceptable if the weight of positive evidence in its favour is too great to put down to chance. In view of the paucity of empirical studies which have been conducted in the subject areas comprising the theory of the firm we are not, regrettably, in a position to adopt a very positive posture towards many of the theories contained in this book. For this reason the approach is essentially impartial, and the reader is left to make up his own mind as to which approach or approaches he personally favours.

Acknowledgement

I would like to express my thanks to the referees who have commented upon various drafts of this book. In particular I would like to thank David Pearce of Leicester University, who has given up so much of his time to assist me with both the present and previous ventures into the publishing field. I wish, however, to retain full responsibility for the contents of this volume.

Part I

The Traditional Theory of the Firm

Chapter 1

The Theory of the Firm in Historical Retrospect

It is appropriate to begin this book with a brief résumé of the development of economic thought relating to the theory of the firm.[1] Deciding where to begin, however, immediately presents problems. Whereas it is universally agreed that the work of Chamberlin and Robinson during the 1930s, to which we will shortly return, constitutes a cohesive theory of the firm, no such agreement exists with respect to the writings of late-nineteenth and early-twentieth century economists. In order to suggest why this is so however, we need to begin with the writings of Adam Smith in 1776, so that the reader can best be left to judge this issue for himself.

Smith was mostly interested in the supply or cost side of a firm's operations [2] since he held that the value of a good was determined by its production cost. He defined this cost to include an appropriate allowance for rents and profit, and was of the opinion that it was in the natural order of things for an entrepreneur to try to maximise his profits by holding down his other costs to a minimum. On the other hand, he did not see this objective as conflicting in any way with a competitive market structure which he expected to develop in almost all industries in the long run. Provided such competition was indeed the order of the day then prices would be determined by costs and hence further analysis of demand conditions became superfluous.

The ascendancy of the proposition that a good's value was directly dependent upon its costs of production lasted broadly until the 1870s. At this time several eminent economists began to reverse the logic of the argument. In their opinion it was not the cost of factors of production which determined a good's value but the value of the good which determined how much the factors of production would be paid. Now the value of a good in this sense clearly depends upon the strength of the demand for it, with the result that the influence of supply upon price became greatly subservient to that of demand. It was further held, especially in England by Jevons,[3] that the strength of the demand for a good depended upon the utility of that good to a prospective buyer, and Jevons re-introduced the notion, long since proposed by Bentham,[4] that the price which a prospective buyer would be prepared to pay for a good would depend upon the utility of that good to the buyer *at the margin*. That is in the light of his previous purchases of the good, if any. Marginal utility was assumed to decline as consumption increased, hence yielding a demand curve falling from left to right. It is worth noting, however, that marginal analysis in the currently more familiar sense of the equating of marginal cost and marginal revenue was not given much attention at this point in time.

Curiously marginal analysis had quite a long history by the 1870s and it is worth a brief detour at this point to introduce the work of Cournot[5] who in a sense put mathematical economics 'on the map', but who personally faded into almost total obscurity for over half a century. Writing in the 1830s Cournot utilised calculus in order to explore the situation of a monopolist, and went on from there to consider duopoly, oligopoly and thence eventually to free competition. He is best remembered for his duopoly model which involved two sellers of spring water (see pp. 41–4) but was himself of the opinion that free competition was much more pervasive in real life. As was true of almost all nineteenth-century economists Cournot retained the objective of profit maximisation, but differed from them in that he specified in mathematical terms how that objective could be attained.

The first real attempt to synthesise the production-cost and utility theories of value is associated with Marshall.[6] In his view value was determined by the forces of supply and demand in more or less equal measure, an opinion adhered to subsequently by all of his successors.

Marshall contributed more than any of his contemporaries to the development of the theory of the firm; for example he refined the utility approach to the derivation of a firm's demand curve and distinguished between the short run and the long run. He also put his training in mathematics to good effect by reviving the work of Cournot, by introducing partial-equilibrium analysis, and by emphasising marginal analysis. It is, however, debatable that Marshall produced a cohesive theory of the firm because his various works are full of inconsistencies.[7]

Opinion would appear to favour the view that Marshall regarded competition as the general rule and monopoly as something of a special case. He recognised that a firm might have access to economies of scale which would produce a downward-sloping average-cost curve, but argued that this would not necessarily produce a trend towards monopolisation because either it might be due to external economies or it might be due to the efforts of an inspired entrepreneur whose successors might not be anything like as efficient.

However, although Marshall showed a clear predilection for competition his concept of 'free' competition diverged appreciably from the concept of 'perfect' competition as we know it today.[8] He recognised both that the actions of individual producers would directly affect those of their rivals, and that producers might be induced to make agreements amongst themselves, neither of which possibilities can be accommodated within the theory of perfect competition. These factors have led several commentators to conclude that Marshall viewed competition as a market construct closely analogous to what is now generally referred to as 'monopolistic' competition. Whatever the truth of the matter it is clear that he regarded duopoly and oligopoly as nothing more than special variants of the monopoly model and hence as unworthy of detailed attention.

The theory of perfect competition was further refined towards its present-day usage by J. M. Clark,[9] but it reached its complete formulation, according to Stigler,[10] only with the publication of Frank Knight's *Risk, Uncertainty and Profit* in 1921. In Stigler's opinion 'It was the meticulous discussion in this work that did most to drive home to economists generally the austere nature of the rigorously defined concept [11] and so prepared the way for the widespread reaction against it in the 1930s.'

The link between Knight's work and the development of monopolistic competition during the 1930s was provided by Sraffa,[12] who pointed out that in many cases firms which operated in a competitive market would find it very difficult to expand output without cutting prices. Hence a firm in competition would not necessarily be faced by an infinitely elastic demand curve.

The prevailing doctrine of economists writing between 1875 and 1925 can therefore be seen to reflect a belief in the empirical validity of the models of competition and monopoly, with the main emphasis upon the former rather than the latter. Although duopoly and oligopoly models were occasionally explored they were generally treated essentially as variants of the monopoly model. Bearing in mind the widespread lack of mathematical expertise among economists during this half-century one may be tempted to advance the cynical view that they preferred to stick to models which were easy to analyse. Certainly, with the honourable exception of Cournot, the almost universally accepted objective of profit maximisation was defined by means other than the equating of marginal cost and marginal revenue. On the other hand, they may genuinely have believed that the typical market was adequately described by the particular variant of the model of competition to which they subscribed, with the model of monopoly held in reserve for markets dominated by a very few sellers.

The major breakthrough in the subject-matter of the theory of the firm is associated with the work of Robinson [13] and Chamberlin [14] during the 1930s.[15] Mrs Robinson's book owed much to Sraffa and can reasonably be regarded as growing out of what had gone before. Chamberlin's work showed more orginality, as he himself was wont to point out, but, for better or for worse, it is current practice to lump them together under the heading of 'the theory of monopolisic competition'. Each work attempted to bridge the gap between the theories of competition and monopoly. The objective of profit maximisation was retained but allowance was expressly made for advertising and product differentiation. Of considerable importance was the use of marginal analysis in the sense of the equating of marginal cost and marginal revenue in order to define the profit-maximising output; this usage has been irrevocably enshrined in all subsequent literature on the theory of the firm.

Unfortunately, the theory of monopolistic competition has been prone to widespread criticism (see pp. 35–7) with the result that it tends to be assigned only a comparatively minor role in any discussion of the theory of the firm. It is curious to note, however, that it currently plays a subservient role to perfect competition despite the fact that it introduced elements of realism, such as product differentiation, sadly lacking in the latter model.

Less attention is also generally paid to monopolistic competition than to the theory of oligopoly. However, as we will go on to argue in a subsequent section (see pp. 39–40), there is no such thing as a *general* theory of oligopoly. Rather, there is a large collection of models containing fairly diverse assumptions which tend to be lumped together willy-nilly under the umbrella title of oligopoly in order to distinguish them from the models of perfect competition and monopoly. Nevertheless, even these variegated models cling to the assumption of profit maximisation and to marginal analysis.

Of course, the truth of the matter may simply be that the real world of the firm is far too complex and diverse for it ever to be approximated to by any one general theory of the firm. Perhaps this explains why, despite their poor showing when tested against data drawn from the real world, the models of perfect competition and monopoly continue to form the mainstay of the theory of the firm. For, in the absence of any replacement model with substantially superior predictive power, it seems not unreasonable to continue to emphasise those models which are highly deterministic and which have survived the test of time.

Chapter 2

Perfect Competition

(i) *The Perfectly Competitive Firm in the Short Run*

In order to construct a model of how firms behave under perfectly competitive conditions we need to begin by making the following set of assumptions:

(*a*) the typical unit of production is a small firm which is both owned and managed by an entrepreneur, and no single firm supplies more than a very small share of total demand for a product;
(*b*) the products of all firms supplying the market are regarded by potential customers as very close substitutes for each other;[1]
(*c*) an individual firm is able to alter its output level without this having any effect upon the price of the product which it sells. The firm is a passive price-taker;
(*d*) the *industry* displays freedom of entry and exit in the sense that there are no impediments upon the ability either of new firms to enter the industry or of existing firms to leave the industry;
(*e*) the sole objective of a firm is to maximise its profits;
(*f*) in order to attain its profit-maximising output a firm equates its marginal cost with its marginal revenue; and
(*g*) both firms and potential customers make decisions in full knowledge of all information which is relevant to those decisions.

Now the assumption that a firm is a price-taker means that price does not vary irrespective of quantity sold. A firm, therefore, faces an infinitely elastic (horizontal) demand curve, and this demand curve is necessarily identical with the firm's average-revenue and marginal-revenue curves.[2]

We can utilise this information on revenues in order to commence the construction of a model depicting a firm's equilibrium position in the short run under conditions of perfect competition. Now, according to our assumptions above, a firm's sole objective is to maximise profit. For the purposes of analysing competitive behaviour we need, however, to clarify the meaning of the term profit by splitting it up into (*a*) normal profit and (*b*) super-normal profit. *Normal profit* is in fact an element of the *costs* to a firm, and is synonymous with the term 'opportunity cost'.[3] It is a payment necessarily provided to factors of production in order to prevent them from choosing to be employed elsewhere, and is equal to the value of a factor in its most profitable alternative usage.

In order to illustrate the meaning of normal profit in the present context we may note that, if an entrepreneur runs his own firm and works full time at his business, he should count the value of his labour as a cost of production because, in effect, it is as much a labour cost as the wages paid to his employees. The precise value which he should place upon his labour is determined by the maximum wage which he could potentially earn while working in any alternative occupation. Likewise, where an entrepreneur sinks his capital into his firm, he should calculate as the true cost of that capital the maximum return which his capital would have earned if invested in any alternative manner. An entrepreneur is therefore earning normal profits when his revenues cover all his costs including the opportunity cost of his time and capital.

Super-normal profit is then most simply defined as any payments accruing to a person or to his assets over and above any payments covered by the term 'normal profit'.

In Figure 2.1 we have superimposed upon the horizontal demand curve a pair of U-shaped average- and marginal-cost curves, with MC cutting AC at the latter's lowest point.[4] Now, as long as marginal revenue exceeds marginal cost (that is to say lies above it in the diagram), an increase in output by one further unit must increase super-normal profit. Hence, if profit is to be maximised, more output should be produced whenever MR exceeds MC. Likewise whenever MC and MR are in equality an expansion of output by one further unit must produce a super-normal loss because MC rises above MR. From this it follows that profit is maximised at output Oq *where marginal cost and marginal revenue are equal.*

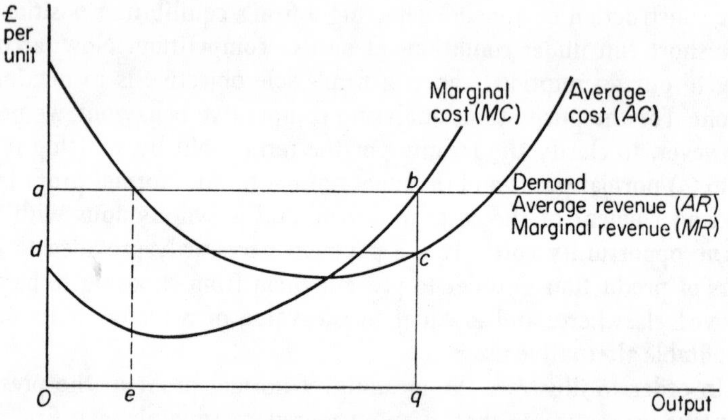

FIG. 2.1 *The perfectly competitive firm in the short run*

At output Oq super-normal profit per unit is equal to average revenue *bq* less average cost *cq*. Total super-normal profit is therefore equal to the area *abcd* (profit per unit *bc* times output *dc*).

It should be borne in mind that not all potentially achievable levels of output are profitable for a firm in Figure 2.1 above. Suppose, for example, that a firm decides to set up in business within a competitive industry, but suffers from long delays in the delivery of some of its machines. This firm may then find itself unable to produce more than a very small output – so small in fact that the firm finds itself making super-normal losses because it is operating over that part of the demand curve (outputs less than Oe) where AC exceeds AR.

This possibility raises the question as to whether or not a firm should operate at all in the short run. Now a firm incurs its fixed costs before actually producing any output. Such costs do not therefore need to be recovered out of the profits in the short run, although they must clearly be recovered by the time the fixed capital falls due for replacement. On the other hand, a firm must pay for its variable factor inputs as and when they are employed in order to ensure that they remain in steady supply. Thus variable costs do need to be covered in the short run, and a firm must either earn sufficient revenue to do so or go out of business altogether.[5] Provided, therefore, that variable costs are being covered a firm should continue to expand production until it is producing that output at which marginal cost and marginal revenue are equated.

(ii) *The Derivation of a Firm's Supply Curve*

Although we have discussed in some detail the demand curve faced by an individual firm in perfect competition, we have not as yet derived the corresponding supply curve. This is done in Figure 2.2.

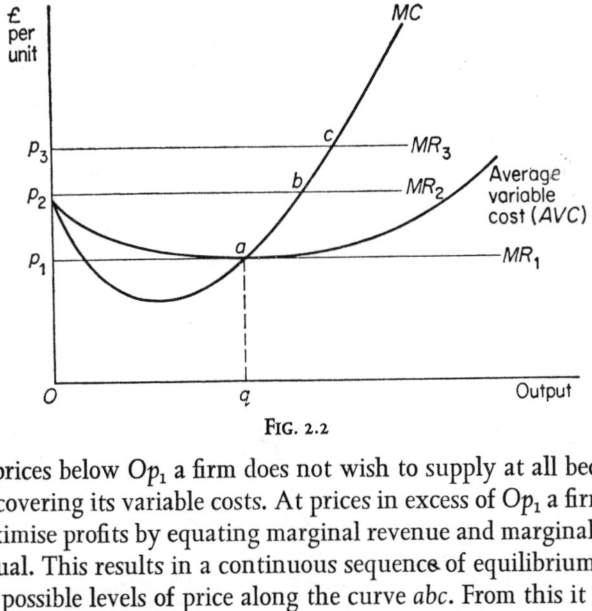

FIG. 2.2

At prices below Op_1 a firm does not wish to supply at all because it is not covering its variable costs. At prices in excess of Op_1 a firm seeks to maximise profits by equating marginal revenue and marginal cost as per usual. This results in a continuous sequence of equilibrium points for all possible levels of price along the curve *abc*. From this it follows that the supply curve of an individual firm under conditions of perfect competition is that part of its marginal-cost curve lying above its average-variable-cost curve.

(iii) *Long-Run Equilibrium in Perfect Competition*

It is possible for a firm to be covering its variable costs in the short run whilst making a super-normal loss per unit. That is to say that at the output determined by the equating of *MC* and *MR*, average cost exceeds average revenue. If this situation continues until such time as the firm's fixed capital wears out, the firm will have to go out of business. But the withdrawal of a firm from the industry curtails total supply and causes price to rise, assuming that demand for the product remains unaltered. In the long run we would therefore expect price to rise steadily in circumstances where firms are in general making short-run super-normal losses and are having to leave the industry when their fixed capital falls due for renewal. This process will continue until price has risen sufficiently for all firms still left in the industry to recover their fixed costs, and hence to earn normal profits, by the time their fixed capital needs to be replaced.

In the opposite situation, in which all firms within an industry are earning super-normal profits in the short run, there is a clear incentive for additional resources to move into the industry, either by way of new firms entering for the first time, or by way of an expansion of output by existing firms. In either event total supply is bound to rise, and price as a consequence to fall, provided demand remains unaltered. We would expect price to fall until it reaches a level at which all firms within the industry are earning only normal profits. Once this is brought about there will be no further incentive for supply to be expanded.

Thus, provided there is freedom of entry into, and exit from, an industry, each firm within the industry can only expect to earn normal

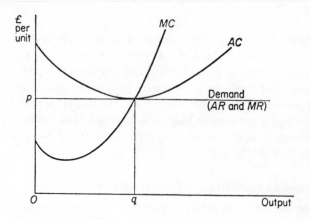

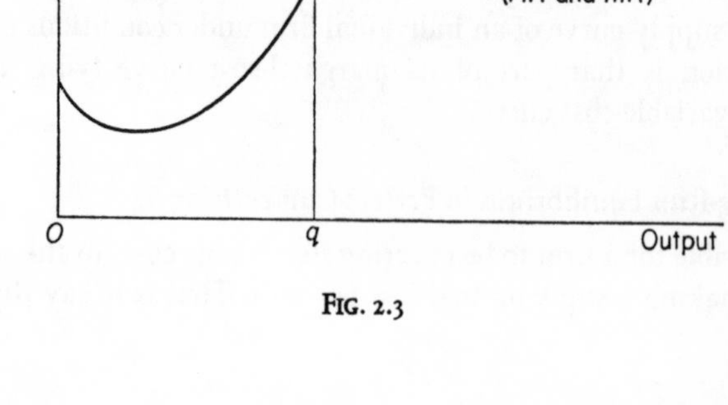

FIG. 2.3

profits in the long run, although super-normal profits and losses may be sustained by such firms in the short run.

Figure 2.3 illustrates the individual firm's long-run equilibrium position. Each firm produces where MC equals MR in order to maximise profits. At that output *Oq*, AC and AR are also equal, and only normal profits are being earned. It is also worth noting that at output *Oq* average cost is at a minimum, indicating that each firm is operating at peak efficiency.

(iv) *The Perfectly Competitive Industry*

In turning our attention from the firm to the industry there are two points worthy of especial note. First, we derive the *industry supply curve* by summing horizontally the supply curves of all firms within the industry. In other words, we add together the total quantity sold by all firms at each relevant price level. Of more importance is the fact that the *industry demand curve* is not horizontal but *falls to the right*, thus joining together the two axes. The reason for this is that, whereas no individual firm can affect price by altering its output level, any substantial alteration in total supply by all firms within the industry taken as a whole must necessarily affect price, with the result that price and output become inversely related.

(v) *Extensions of the Model: The Cobweb Theorem*

When we illustrate the cost and revenue conditions for a firm in equilibrium at a single point in time we refer to this as a *static* model. When, further, we compare the cost and revenue conditions of the same firm at two separate points in time this is known as *comparative statics*. The standard model of perfect competition is, therefore, a comparative-static model because it illustrates the equilibrium position of a firm both in the short and in the long run. All comparative-static models suffer, however, from one major drawback, in that they neither describe the sequence of events by which a firm moves from one equilibrium position to the next, nor is there any way of knowing whether any particular equilibrium position will ever be reached. This is especially true of a long-run equilibrium where the long run is ill-defined.

To overcome these difficulties it is necessary to analyse *market dynamics* which encompass not merely equilibrium situations but the disequilibria which exist between such situations. In subsequent sections of this book we will be considering dynamic growth models of the firm (see pp. 118–22). It is possible, however, to develop a simple dynamic variant of the model of perfect competition, known as the *cobweb theorem.*

In Figure 2.4 we have an initial equilibrium situation of price OA and output OX. Assuming that output cannot be varied in the short run any increase in demand (illustrated by a shift of the demand curve upwards and to the right) can only be met by a rise in price, for example the combination OC and OX. The question then arises as to how the sellers will react to this price rise. If they expect it to be a transitory phenomenon they will clearly carry on producing as before. But if they expect the higher price to remain in force they will decide to increase their output to the level OZ, which is the point on the supply curve appropriate to a price of OC. In fact, however, the correct equilibrium situation once demand has shifted from D to D^1 is price OB and output OY. This suggests that producers take decisions about how much to produce in the forthcoming time period in ignorance of the price which will actually hold in the market, and as a result are unable to sell all that they produce at the anticipated price.

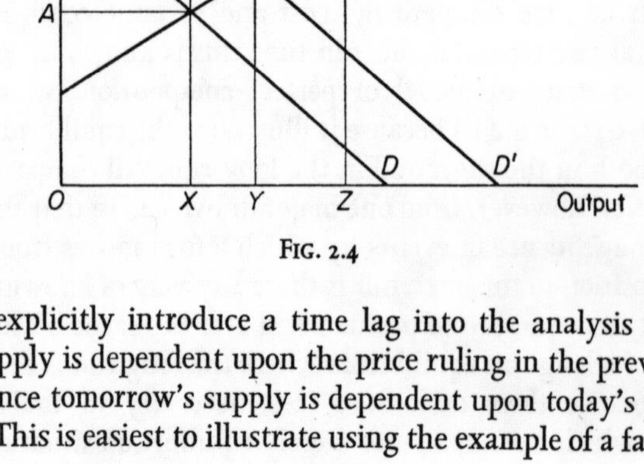

FIG. 2.4

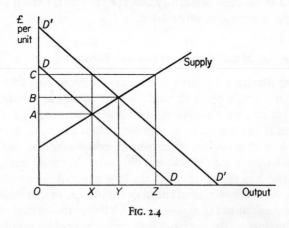

Let us explicitly introduce a time lag into the analysis such that today's supply is dependent upon the price ruling in the previous time period (hence tomorrow's supply is dependent upon today's price, and so forth). This is easiest to illustrate using the example of a farmer who plants a crop once a year. We will also assume that once the decision has been made as to the forthcoming year's output this is to be treated as unalterable, and that once the crop has been harvested it will be sold in its entirety to the highest bidder.

Using Figure 2.5 let us suppose that price is initially *OC*. On this basis farmers will want to supply S_1 next year. But if S_1 is actually put on the market during the second year it will only fetch a price of *OA*, equivalent to point D_1 on the demand curve. Hence, whereas the farmers expect a better than the equilibrium price, they actually receive a less than the equilibrium price. But at the new price of *OA* farmers will only want to supply S_2 during the third year, and this will sell at a greater than the equilibrium price of *OB* corresponding to point D_2 on the demand curve. The farmers will decide on the basis of this price to produce S_3 during the fourth year, and so on.

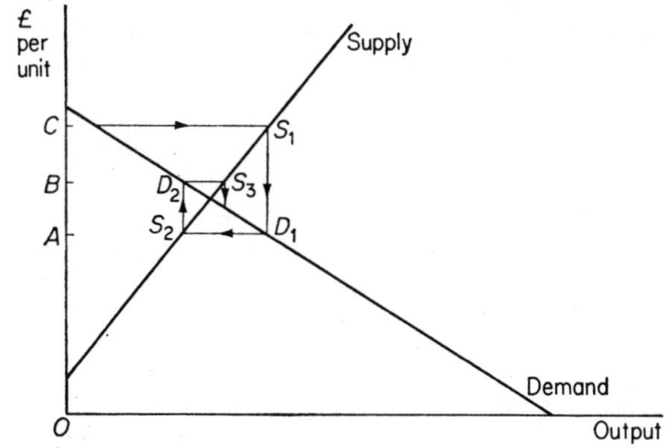

FIG. 2.5

If we consider the variation of market price over time we can see that it alternates above and below the equilibrium price, although it is steadily moving closer to it. The action of the farmers can thus be said to be stabilising the market. It is, however, quite possible for the farmers to act in a destabilising manner, as is illustrated in Figure 2.6. In this diagram we can clearly see that the adjustment process is such as to cause price to diverge ever further from its equilibrium level.

The cobweb theorem involves two basic adjustment processes. First, there is the adjustment by producers of output in the light of the previously established price. Secondly, there is the adjustment of price to

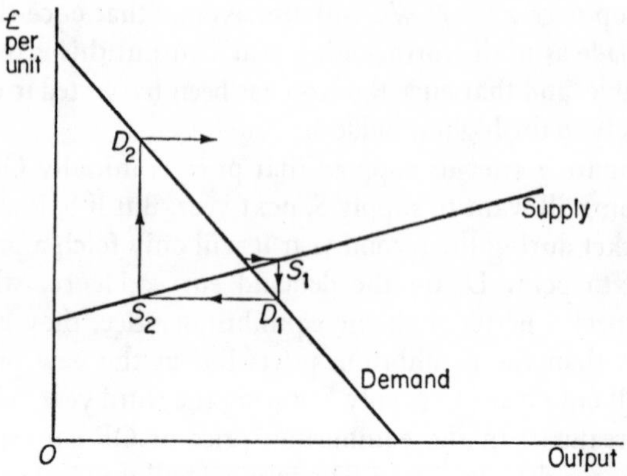

FIG. 2.6

this new level of output. Unfortunately, this model, though useful for illustrating in a simple way the characteristics of stability and instability in a dynamic context, suffers from a lack of realism in that producers are assumed never to learn from experience. It is unreasonable to assume, especially in the destabilising case, that producers will fail to realise that their output decisions have a fundamental effect upon price. But if they do realise that this is so they will clearly take the necessary steps to ensure that they retain greater control over the market by adjusting supply in a more subtle way than that postulated in the cobweb theorem.

(vi) *Criticisms of the Model*

The model of perfect competition is subject to one overriding criticism, which refers to its inability to tell us anything useful about the real world. The model has become so refined over the years that its mathematical precision has few (if any) peers in the social sciences. Unfortunately, its assumptions are so restrictive that it is hard to see its relevance in a highly developed capitalist economy. Organised markets such as the Stock Exchange and the various commodity exchanges fit the model quite well, as possibly does the agricultural industry. But non-homogeneous manufactured products do not fit the model at all well. The model therefore has very little to contribute to industrial economics except (for policy purposes) as an ideal structure for an industry against which to compare those found in practice,[6] and even there the assumption that perfect competition is ideal from a social point of view has come under fierce attack. As Chamberlin has put it [7]

> The explicit recognition that product is differentiated brings into the open the problem of variety and makes it clear that *pure competition may no longer be regarded as in any sense an 'ideal' for purposes of welfare economics*. In many cases it would be quite impossible to establish it, even supposing it to be desirable ... But even where possible it would not be desirable to standardise products beyond a certain point.[8]

Chapter 3

Workable Competition

Dissatisfaction with the ability of the model of perfect competition to act as an ideal market structure for policy purposes led to various attempts to replace it with the operationally more valid concept of *workable competition*. This phrase originated with J. M. Clark [1] who argued that perfect competition 'does not and cannot exist, and has presumably never existed'. He therefore set out to develop alternative criteria to those of perfect competition for use in assessing how well competition is working.

There is now a substantial literature on the topic of workable competition.[2] Scherer has provided an outline of some criteria of workability of competition as follows.[3]

Structural Norms include the following:

(1) The number of traders should be at least as large as scale economies permit.
(2) There should be no artificial inhibitions on mobility and entry.
(3) There should be moderate and price-sensitive quality differentials in the products offered.

Conduct criteria include:

(4) Some uncertainty should exist in the minds of rivals as to whether price initiatives will be followed.

(5) Firms should strive to achieve their goals independently, without collusion.
(6) There should be no unfair, exclusionary, predatory, or coercive tactics.
(7) Inefficient suppliers and customers should not be shielded permanently.
(8) Sales promotion should not be misleading.
(9) Persistent, harmful price discrimination should be absent.

Last, we have a number of *performance criteria*:

(10) Firm's production operations should be efficient.
(11) Promotional expenses should not be excessive.
(12) Profits should be at levels just sufficient to reward investment, efficiency and innovation.
(13) Output levels and the range of qualities should be responsive to consumer demands.
(14) Opportunities for introducing technically superior new products and processes should be exploited.
(15) Prices should not intensify cyclical instability.
(16) Success should accrue to sellers who best serve consumer wants.

Scherer goes on to note, however, that the above list begs a large number of questions. He therefore concludes that[4] 'it is difficult to state *a priori* how we formulate hard-and-fast rules for identifying cases in which a departure from competition is desirable'.

Chapter 4

Monopoly

(i) *Monopoly in the Short Run and in the Long Run*

A monopoly is held to exist where a firm is the sole supplier of a particular good or service. Such a firm therefore has no existing competitors, and is protected by barriers to entry (see pp. 71–82) from the encroachment into its markets of potential competitors.

Control over its markets enables a monopoly to operate rather differently from a competitive firm. Most importantly the absence of competitors means that a monopoly cannot be undersold, and it can therefore vary its selling price at will as an alternative strategy to variations in its output level. This does not imply, however, that demand is completely insensitive to price variations (that is has zero elasticity). A monopoly which serves the whole market for any given product is clearly faced by a demand curve which represents total market demand for this product, and which will therefore slope downwards to the right in the usual way. Hence any alteration in price must produce a change in quantity demanded of opposite sign.

A monopolist (assumed to be the sole decision-taker, or entrepreneur, in his firm) is therefore able either to fix his price and to sell as much as the market will absorb at that price, or he can decide to sell a specific quantity of output and obtain the best price he can for it. In either case the objective of the exercise is always to maximise his profits, and this he achieves by selecting that price–output combination indicated by the application of the decision rule that marginal cost should be equated with marginal revenue.

The monopoly model thus has several things in common with the model of perfect competition discussed above. Both models specify that decisions are taken by an entrepreneur, that the objective is to maximise profits, and that this objective is achieved through the application of marginal analysis. Finally we may note that the assumption of perfect knowledge is common to both models, although perfect knowledge arises in the monopoly model as a result of the fact that the only relevant cost information is generated by the monopoly itself, and also from the fact that a monopolist can determine the elasticity of the market demand curve simply by varying his price and seeing what happens to output.

Unlike the competitive model, however, the monopoly model does not have a supply curve. Now a supply curve is merely a hypothetical representation of what a producer would like to sell at different price levels. In the case of monopoly the monopolist always pre-selects his most profitable price–output combination and is not willing to sell at any other price. This price–output combination is represented by a single point on the demand curve, so that in monopoly we have what is known as *point supply*.

The monopoly model is depicted in Figure 4.1 (p. 22). The average-revenue and demand curves are treated as synonymous as per usual. Now it can readily be proven that the marginal-revenue curve corresponding to any linear average-revenue curve which falls to the right will cut the horizontal axis midway to the point at which that axis is bisected by the average-revenue curve. For this reason *MR* is necessarily smaller in value than AR at all possible levels of output (whereas *MR* was necessarily *equal* to AR in the case of a competitive firm).[1] This results from the fact that if the monopolist lowers his price on all units for sale in order to expand output by one further unit, he will, as a result, be losing some revenue on all of the units which he could have sold at the original higher price level, as well as gaining some additional revenue from the extra unit sold. The extent to which AR and *MR* will diverge depends upon the elasticity of the demand curve at the price levels in question. It is also worth remembering that marginal revenue can be negative in value even at output levels where average revenue is positive.

It is customary to incorporate U-shaped average- and marginal-cost curves into the monopoly model. We would, however, expect the monopolist's cost curves to fall more sharply over the initial range of output levels than would be true of each of a large number of small firms supplying the same output overall. This largely reflects the much greater capitalisation (fixed costs) which we would expect to find in a firm which intends to supply the whole of, rather than only a small part of, the market. We would also expect a monopolist to have access to other sources of scale economies which are unavailable to a small competitive firm. On the other hand, we would expect a monopolist's average-cost curve eventually to rise quite sharply, first because the average productivity of his factors of production is bound to decline as increasingly more of them are purchased (implying that ever greater quantities of factor inputs need to be purchased in order to obtain a unit increase in output), and secondly because he will be buying factor services on such a large scale that he must in the process force their price up sharply against himself.

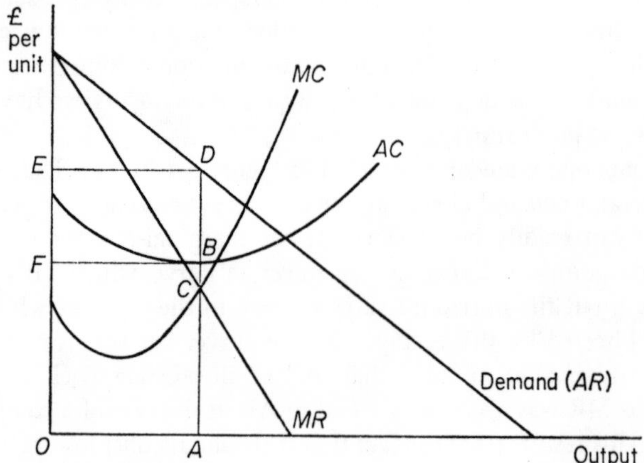

FIG. 4.1

We can therefore illustrate the basic monopoly model in the light of the above discussion of its revenue and cost conditions. The monopolist equates marginal revenue with marginal cost in order to determine his profit-maximising output (OA in Figure 4.1). However, in order to discover the selling price, we must extend the vertical up from point A through the intersection of MC and MR at C until it reaches the average-revenue curve at D. This yields a price of OE per unit sold. The average cost per unit sold is given by *AB* so that the monopolist is making super-normal profits (as previously defined) of *BD* per unit. This yields a total super-normal profit equivalent to the area *BDEF*.

Note, however, that this is both the *short-run and the long-run* equilibrium price–output combination for the monopolist. Potential competitors are excluded from entry into the industry so that there is basically no reason to expect any changes in the monopolist's cost and revenue conditions even over extended periods of time. Thus, unlike a firm in perfect competition, a monopolist can retain super-normal profits even in the long run.

(ii) *Extensions of the Model: Price Discrimination*

The basic monopoly model can usefully be extended in order to analyse price discrimination. Price discrimination occurs when a producer sells a particular commodity to at least two different buyers at varying prices, even though each unit of the commodity is produced at the same cost.

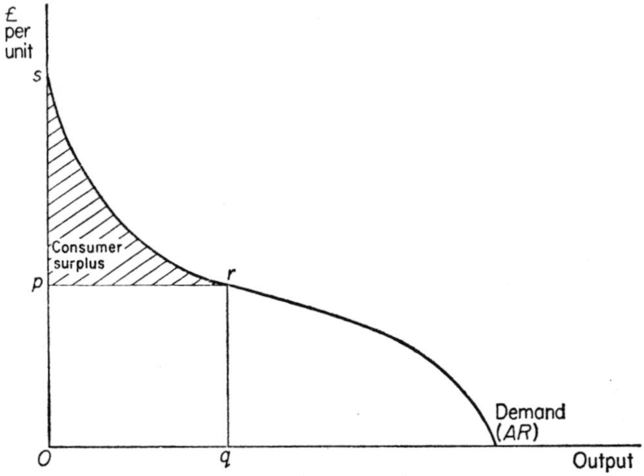

FIG. 4.2

The underlying rationale for price discrimination is that different buyers may be willing to pay varying amounts for an identical good or service, and it may prove profitable for the seller to take advantage of this fact. The basic model is illustrated in Figure 4.2.

At price *Op* the marginal buyer is willing to purchase the *q*th unit of output. However the shape of the demand curve indicates that there are other purchasers willing, if necessary, to go as high as a price of *Os* in order to obtain the product. Therefore, if all purchasers are charged the standard price of *Op*, the monopolist is effectively forgoing the opportunity to obtain the revenue indicated by the area *prs*, known as the *consumer surplus*, which he would be able to acquire were he in a position to charge each purchaser the maximum price per unit which that purchaser is willing to pay.

Successful discrimination generally rests both upon the ability of the seller to select his clientele, and upon the prevention of resale from the customer who buys cheaply to the customer who pays a relatively high price. Since it is extremely difficult to resell most services it is much easier to practise price discrimination in the services as against the goods sector. It is also considerably easier to discriminate if markets are physically separated, such as home and foreign markets. In the latter circumstances the monopolist is discriminating only between a few, large, markets, as is also true where, for example, a firm sells part of its production to another manufacturer for incorporation in his output, and part direct to the general public at much higher prices (for example car parts). It is also possible, however, for a monopolist to discriminate on an individual basis, for example a lawyer can charge different amounts to his various clients in return for representing them in court since the service rendered is specific to the individual and hence cannot be resold.

The positive benefits to the monopolist are as follows:

(1) For any given level of output, any form of discrimination enables a monopolist to acquire for himself part of the consumer surplus which would be denied him were he to sell his entire output at the same price; and

(2) A monopolist never finds it profitable to produce beyond the output level at which marginal cost and marginal revenue are brought into equality. But the effect of successful discrimination is to flatten the slope of the marginal-revenue curve, because MR must fall more slowly as output is expanded where the monopolist is obtaining part of the consumer surplus for himself. As a result, it becomes profitable to

expand output beyond the single selling price equilibrium because the unchanged marginal-cost curve necessarily cuts the flattened marginal-revenue curve at a higher output level.

It is a relatively simple matter to explore the economic principles involved in successful price discrimination using the model illustrated in Figure 4.3. This model incorporates a monopolist operating in two markets both of which are characterised by imperfect competition. It is, however, an extremely simple matter to interchange one of the markets with a perfectly competitive market, or indeed to add on as many additional markets to the model as we so wish, since the economic principles involved will in either case remain unchanged.

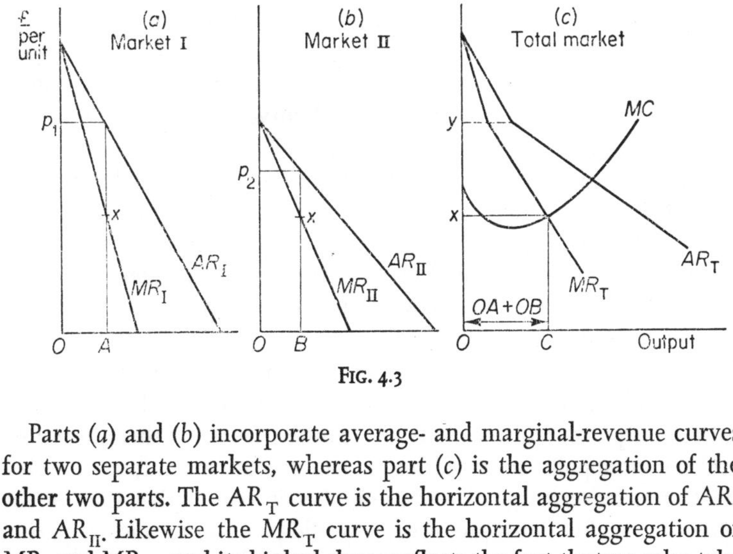

FIG. 4.3

Parts (*a*) and (*b*) incorporate average- and marginal-revenue curves for two separate markets, whereas part (*c*) is the aggregation of the other two parts. The AR_T curve is the horizontal aggregation of AR_I and AR_{II}. Likewise the MR_T curve is the horizontal aggregation of MR_I and MR_{II}, and its kinked shape reflects the fact that no sales take place in Market II yielding a marginal revenue in excess of O*y*. The marginal-cost curve appears only in part (*c*). This is because costs of production are assumed not to vary irrespective of where the goods are sold (the logic of the model remaining unaffected by differences in transport costs), so that MC applies only to *total* sales.

In order to determine his profit-maximising output the monopolist equates MC and MR_T. This yields an output of OC. The monopolist's next task is to decide where to sell this output in the sense of allocating it to best advantage over the two markets which he serves. This is achieved where output is allocated in such a way as to *keep marginal revenue equal in both markets* (at a level of Ox). Thus we find that he should sell a quantity OA in Market I and quantity OB in Market II, where OA + OB equals total sales of OC.

Now let us consider what the monopolist has been doing in economic terms since this should help to clarify why he has acted in the manner indicated above.

The monopolist has two markets to serve. Each time that he intends expanding output by one further unit he must consider in which market to sell it. Since it costs the same to produce irrespective of where it is sold, the incremental unit of output should logically be sold in whichever market offers the greater addition to revenue, that is the greater marginal revenue. Thus if marginal revenue is greater in one market than in the other, that is the market in which the good should be sold. But marginal revenue necessarily declines as output expands in any market because the *MR* curve falls to the right. As a result expanding output in one market alone must cause marginal revenue in that market eventually to fall below that ruling in the other market. Hence where a monopolist has a limited output to sell (such as OC in Figure 4.3 (*c*)), he should switch from one market to the other according to where marginal revenue is currently greater, and by so doing he ends up in the above example by supplying OA to one market and OB to the other.

Now the logical implication of the above argument is that the monopolist must derive as much additional revenue from selling the final unit of output in one market as in the other. Clearly if this was not so, and the monopolist intended initially to allocate his output in such a way as to leave marginal revenue higher in one market than in the other for the final unit produced, it would pay him to transfer part of his output from the market where the marginal revenue was relatively low to the market where it was relatively high. Furthermore, he should continue to do this only up to the point where the marginal revenue in both markets is equated, since beyond that point further transfers of output would cause total profits to fall.

This does *not*, however, imply that selling price ends up the same in both markets, as can be seen from Figure 4.3. If the two sets of average-revenue and marginal-revenue curves are identical then clearly the equating of marginal revenue in each market produces identical sales levels and hence identical prices. But if the demand curves are dissimilar, which is to say that the elasticity of demand is different in each market at any given price level, the equating of marginal revenue in each market produces dissimilar sales levels and hence different prices. It is thus a precondition for profitable discrimination that the elasticity of demand should not be the same at any given price level in all markets served.

Thus the rationale for discriminatory behaviour is that the monopolist sells only to those people in each market willing to pay the highest prices for his goods. Were he to sell in only one market he would also be obliged to sell to customers who do not value his goods very highly and, since price would have to be the same for all customers, it would have to be set at an appropriately low level.

(iii) *Criticisms of the Model*

The term 'monopoly power' is in such common usage that one might be forgiven for thinking that pure monopolies are frequently to be found in the real world. It is interesting to note, therefore, that by far the strongest indictment of the monopoly model comes by way of an accusation that there are *no* pure monopolies to be found in the real world. Underlying this assertion is the belief that there is no such thing as a non-competing product because everything has some kind of substitute, no matter how imperfect. The acquisition of monopoly supply largely stems from the existence of a system of patenting new products, but however ingenious and desirable a new product may turn out to be, there is bound to be something else which can be used, if absolutely necessary, in its place.

It is often pointed out that the nationalised industries are all monopoly suppliers of one type of good or service. However, even these industries fall into two main groups, namely 'power' and 'transport', and all of the industries within each group compete quite fiercely with one another.

The monopoly model is of some utility as a limiting case of market behaviour with which more complex theories of the firm can be compared, especially with respect to the relative accuracy of their respective predictions about market behaviour. This is, however, rather scant justification for the effort devoted to the refinement of a model with negligible grounding in the realities of industrial organisation. It is therefore worthwhile at this point to consider the evidence about concentration levels in order to assess just how valid is the criticism of the monopoly model expressed above.

(iv) *The Extent of Monopoly Power*

In taking stock of the data which can be used, albeit with caution, to determine the extent of monopoly power within the United Kingdom the first thing to appreciate is that true monopoly in the textbook sense of a single seller is, to all intents and purposes, non-existent. Furthermore, those product markets which are almost wholly supplied by a single seller tend to be too small to shed much light upon the prevalence of monopoly power in industry generally, and are anyway often characterised by appreciable monopoly power on the buying side.

This information does not, however, destroy the validity of the monopoly model. Where, for example, there are several large sellers in a product market they may act in collusion and hence adopt the same price–output combination as would a single seller. The purpose of this section, therefore, is to consider data on industrial concentration in order to assess the prevalence of monopoly power.

It is customary to utilise the *concentration ratio* as a proxy for monopoly power.[2] This ratio measures the proportion of U.K. sales, value-added, employment or assets accounted for by a small number of leading firms within an industry. The basic data is drawn from the five-yearly Census of Production. The latest Census to take place was that of 1973. This data has not, however, been published as yet, so that the latest set of figures currently used to determine concentration levels comes from the 1968 Census. A vast quantity of literature exists concerning concentration levels but we will restrict ourselves to that which is most up to date and comprehensive, namely the publications of the National Institute of Economic and Social Research [3] and those of Utton [4] and Aaronovitch and Sawyer.[5]

The use of Census of Production data is admittedly subject to many limitations for the purposes of estimating concentration ratios.[6] It is also sometimes argued that a simple three-, four-, or five-firm concentration ratio does not accurately reflect the extent of monopoly power. In several studies attempts have been made to overcome this latter deficiency by supplementing the concentration ratio with further information about the relative sizes of other firms within an industry. Evely and Little, for example, in their seminal work based upon data drawn from the 1951 Census of Production, employed the 'size ratio of units' which measured the 'average size of the three largest units relative to the average size of other units in the trade'.[7] In Walshe's opinion, however,[8] 'it is quite reasonable to expect that a firm with a 70 per cent market share, or a duopoly with an 80 per cent market share, or a triopoly with a 90 per cent market share has some degree of monopoly or near-monopoly power, which can be exercised within constraints', and he himself uses as a criterion of monopoly power a five-firm sales concentration ratio of over 90 per cent.[9]

It is clear from all of the studies referred to above that the level of market concentration has been increasing quite rapidly since the 1950s. Aaronovitch and Sawyer have calculated *average* five-firm concentration ratios as shown in Table 4.1.[10]

TABLE 4.1 *Average five-firm concentration ratios*

Year	Per cent
1935	52·0*
1951	55·8
1958	58·7
1963	63·5
1968	69·0
1974	76·0*

* rough estimates

According to Walshe a total of forty-four product groups which had sales of over £10 million in 1963 exceeded a five-firm 90 per cent concentration ratio. These represented some 14 per cent of the total sales of principal products [11] of all manufacturing industries reported in the 1963 Census, a figure which he refers to as 'clearly not insignificant'.[12]

Aaronovitch and Sawyer also analysed the 1968 Census of Production in order to produce a distribution of five-firm concentration ratios. Their results appear as shown in Table 4.2.[13]

It would seem fairly apparent from the above that in many industries it would be a relatively simple matter for the dominant firms to get together in order to exercise their combined monopoly power. Whether or not they take advantage of this opportunity is, of course, a matter which can only be resolved by extensive enquiries on an industry-by-industry basis. Such collusion would contravene the antimonopoly legislation, but cases investigated by the Monopolies Commission suggest that this is not often a strong deterrent.[14]

TABLE 4.2 *Distribution of five-firm ratios (based on sales) 1968*

Concentration ratio Per cent	No. of industries	Share of sales Per cent
0–10	0	0·0
10–20	8	2·5
20–30	20	4·7
30–40	27	8·9
40–50	34	9·7
50–60	45	12·7
60–70	35	12·7
70–80	39	9·3
80–90	46	9·6
90–100	70	29·9
	324	100·0

Our general conclusion must therefore be that if one accepts a five-firm concentration ratio of over 90 per cent as a proxy for monopoly power then such power is quite pervasive, even if there is no real evidence of monopolies in the strict textbook sense of the word. On the other hand, the bulk of the industries examined appear to fall somewhere between the extremes of monopoly and perfect competition, and it is to these industries that we must now turn our attention.

Chapter 5

Monopolistic Competition

(1) *The Model of Monopolistic Competition*

The model of monopolistic competition retains many of the assumptions of the model of perfect competition, but differs from it in one major respect. Whereas the industry is assumed to consist of a large number of small firms each of which is run by an entrepreneur who pursues the goal of profit maximisation using marginal analysis under conditions of perfect knowledge, and whereas there is freedom of entry into, and exit out of, the industry, each firm can no longer be treated as a price-taker. This stems from the fact that each firm produces a product which is regarded by consumers as being in some meaningful way different from the products made by all other producers. Such differences between products may be either real or imagined, but this distinction is unimportant provided that consumers treat the products of different firms as being less than perfect substitutes for one another.

Considerable importance is placed upon the assumption that no individual producer is in a position to supply more than an insignificant share of the total market, because this implies that other firms within the industry remain more or less unaffected by any action taken by an individual producer. This allows an individual producer considerable scope in pursuing independent policies, which will normally fall into one of three categories. A producer can alter either his price, the extent to which he promotes his product, or the degree to which his product is differentiated from all others on the market. In these respects he behaves more like a monopolist than a firm in perfect competition, since the latter is a price-taker and does not indulge in sales promotion because it can already sell as much as it can produce at the ruling market price.

In order to simplify the analysis it is helpful to make certain additional assumptions at this point. These are (1) that each firm has already decided upon the optimal degree of product differentiation and extent of sales promotion, which allows us to concentrate solely upon the effects of price changes upon profits, and (2) that each firm operates along identical cost and revenue functions.[1]

In Figure 5.1 we have drawn two demand curves, the first of which (*DD*) demonstrates what will happen to an individual firm's sales when any price change instituted by it is exactly matched by its competitors, and the second of which (*dd*) demonstrates what will happen to an individual firm's sales when any price change instituted by it is *not* matched by its competitors.

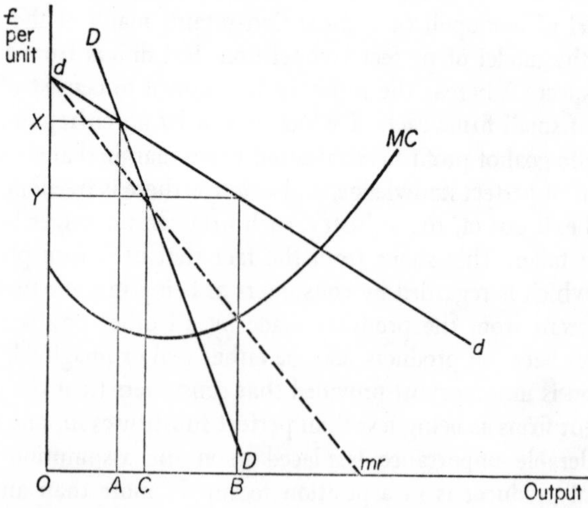

FIG. 5.1

The firm is initially in equilibrium at a price OX selling OA units. It then decides to try and maximise its profits by equating marginal cost and marginal revenue in the expectation that other firms *will not respond.* The relevant demand curve is thus *dd* and the firm equates MC and *mr* to produce at a price of OY and a *desired* output of OB. But if all firms within the industry operate along identical revenue and cost curves in pursuit of an identical objective, and all are equally well informed about the market, they will all simultaneously alter price by an equivalent amount. As a result each firm *in practice* finds itself operating along demand curve DD, where at a price of OY sales amount to only OC units and profits are *not* being maximised.

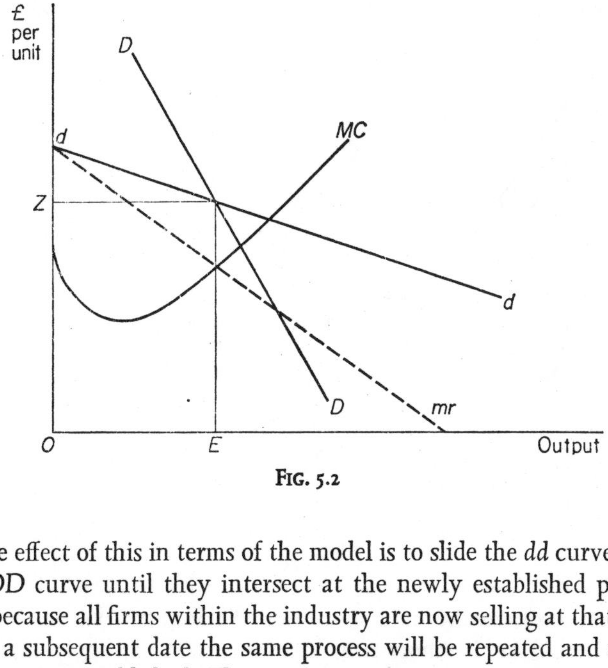

FIG. 5.2

The effect of this in terms of the model is to slide the *dd* curve down the DD curve until they intersect at the newly established price of OY, because all firms within the industry are now selling at that price.

At a subsequent date the same process will be repeated and a new, lower, price established. This sequence of successive price cuts will, however, not come to a halt until the conditions necessary for short-run equilibrium, as set out in Figure 5.2, are achieved. Here the equating of MC and *mr* produces a price of OZ and an output of OE. This is the *short-run equilibrium* for each firm because each firm is now *in practice* maximising its profits, and therefore has no further incentive to alter price in order to improve its profits at the expense of its rivals. (Profits will, however, only be positive provided that average revenue exceeds average cost at output OE.)

In the long run the assumption that firms can freely enter or leave the industry comes into play. If we assume that firms already within the industry are making super-normal profits in the short run, which is the usual case, then this will attract new firms into the industry over time and hence expand total supply. One result of this influx of new firms is to cut the market share held by any individual firm, which is the same thing as shifting the *DD* curve to the left in Figure 5.2. At the same time new firms extend the range of product differentiation and this weakens the preference of customers for any single producer's goods, with the result that the *DD* curve becomes flatter (more elastic at any given price level).

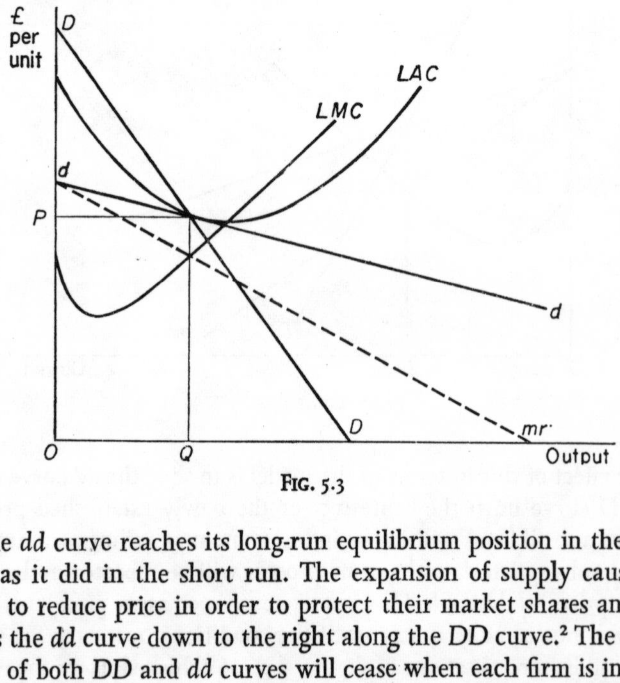

FIG. 5.3

The *dd* curve reaches its long-run equilibrium position in the same way as it did in the short run. The expansion of supply causes all firms to reduce price in order to protect their market shares and this shifts the *dd* curve down to the right along the *DD* curve.[2] The movement of both *DD* and *dd* curves will cease when each firm is in long-run equilibrium as depicted in Figure 5.3. Here we have drawn in the firm's long-run average- and marginal-cost curves. The *LAC* is tangential to *dd* at the point of intersection of the *DD* and *dd* curves. The output level of OQ units appropriate to that intersection is also that appropriate to the intersection of the *LMC* and *mr* curves.[3] This output level represents a long-run equilibrium because each firm is maximising its profits (LMC=*mr*) while at the same time each firm is earning only normal profits (AR=LAC) so that there is no further tendency for firms to enter or leave the industry.

We can therefore see that in long-run equilibrium the firm under monopolistic competition differs from the firm under perfect competition in that (1) price is higher and output is lower, and (2) average cost is not at its minimum level. This latter difference stems from the fact that the demand curve facing a monopolistically competitive firm is downward sloping rather than horizontal as in perfect competition. Despite this difference, however, the firm in long-run equilibrium earns only normal profits in both models.

(ii) *Criticisms of the Model*

(*a*) *Methodological*

The methodological underpinnings of the theory of monopolistic competition have been widely criticised. In particular there has been a protracted discussion in the literature concerning the definition of the group of firms who are in monopolistic competition. This problem arises because products made by each firm are to some degree differentiated from all others. In his seminal work Chamberlin [4] referred to the 'group' of competing firms as follows:

The group contemplated is one which would *ordinarily* be regarded as composing one imperfectly competitive market: a number of automobile manufacturers, of producers of pots and pans, of magazine publishers, or of retail shoe dealers. From our point of view, each producer within the group is a monopolist, yet his market is interwoven with those of his competitors, and he is no longer to be isolated from them.

This definition evoked a strong response from Stigler who argued that: [5]

It is perfectly possible, on Chamberlin's picture of economic life, that the group contain only one firm, or, on the contrary, that it include all of the firms in the economy. This latter possibility can readily follow from the asymmetry of substitution relationships among firms: taking any one product as our point of departure, each substitute has in turn its substitutes, so that the adjacent cross-elasticities may not diminish, and even increase, as we move farther away from the 'base' firm in some technological or geographical sense.

As Cohen and Cyert point out [6]

Chamberlin's problem in defining the group is unavoidable. On the one hand he assumes that each firm is a monopolist, which implies that there is a low cross-elasticity of demand [7] among the products of the group. On the other hand he assumes that the group is closely interdependent, which implies that there is a high cross-elasticity of demand among the products of the group.

Because of this difficulty, Chamberlin, as we saw in our analysis of the model above, introduced what Stigler referred to as the *uniformity* assumption [8] by proceeding 'under the heroic assumption that both demand and cost curves for all the "products" are uniform throughout the group'.[9] Chamberlin also introduced the assumption that 'any adjustment of price or of "product" by a single producer spreads its influence over so many of his competitors that the impact felt by any one is negligible and does not lead him to any readjustment of his own situation'.[10] This Stigler called the *symmetry* assumption.[11]

Stigler went on to argue that the uniformity assumption implies physically homogeneous products and hence, by implication, when taken in conjunction with the assumption of perfect knowledge, infinitely elastic demand curves.[12] Furthermore, when the symmetry assumption is also taken into account, the only possible interrelationship between products is, in Stigler's view,[13] that of close substitutability.

Admittedly Chamberlin did relax the uniformity assumption in the course of his book in order to allow for the possibility of super-normal profits in equilibrium. In Stigler's view, however, 'in the general case we cannot make a single statement about economic events in the world we sought to analyse. It is true that many such statements are made by Chamberlin, but none follows rigorously from the ambiguous apparatus. . . . And so the first attempt has failed.' [14]

Over the years a considerable debate has taken place in the literature with respect to the Chamberlin model.[15] This debate is too complex to merit further detailed discussion at this point, although we will return in the final section below to consider the over-all value of the model. Meanwhile we must turn briefly to consider the debate about the existence or otherwise of excess capacity.

(b) *Excess Capacity*

We have seen in the model of long-run equilibrium for a firm in monopolistic competition that the resultant output level is less than that at which *LRAC* is at a minimum. In perfect competition, however, each firm produces that output at which *LRAC* is at its lowest level. It is therefore argued that monopolistic competition is characterised by excess capacity.

The debate concerning the existence or otherwise of excess capacity was opened by Harrod [16] who took the view that 'imperfect competition does not usually tend to create excess capacity'.[17] The crux of his argument was that the Chamberlin model needed to be amended in order to allow for the possibility that producers make proper allowance for the likelihood of subsequent entry into the industry of additional firms when choosing their profit-maximising output in the short run. Harrod argued that firms would forgo some potential short-run profits in order to discourage entry of new firms, and that consequently the demand curve facing each firm in the long run would be flatter than under Chamberlin's assumptions. Since the long-run marginal-revenue curve would also be flatter the intersection of long-run marginal cost and marginal revenue would occur at a greater output level than in the Chamberlin model and thus eliminate some, but not all,[18] of the excess capacity.

Other critiques [19] of the excess-capacity prediction have also involved modifications of Chamberlin's model. This has led Cohen and Cyert [20] to conclude that 'when they quarrel with the excess capacity implications of monopolistic competition, Harrod and the other critics are really developing their own models of imperfect competition rather than analysing the properties of Chamberlin's model'.

(iii) *Assessment of the Model*

There is a fairly fundamental disagreement amongst commentators as to the value of the model of monopolistic competition. We have already noted Stigler's searching criticisms,[21] although these have not gone unanswered. The assertion that the model yields no testable hypotheses was voiced by Archibald when he wrote that [22] 'in the case of the individual firm, with advertising and quality variation, the reason is that significant predictions cannot be obtained without more information than is usually assumed or readily available. In the case of the group, even without advertising and quality variation, the reason is that the demand relations of the theory are inadequately specified.' This viewpoint was endorsed by Friedman [23] who adjudged the model 'incompetent to contribute to the analysis of a host of important problems'. Likewise Cohen and Cyert [24] have gone on record with the claim that 'the model of monopolistic competition is not a useful addition to economic theory because it does not describe any market in the real world. We take this position on both empirical and theoretical grounds.' They feel that monopolistic competition cannot be anything more than a transitory phenomenon, and suggest that industries commonly associated with monopolistic competition can more appropriately be analysed using the models of monopoly and oligopoly.[25] Hadar [26] set out to refute Archibald's claim that 'the difficulties of the "qualitative calculus" applied to maximising models of the firm are too great to overcome'.[27] He concluded that 'it is possible to specify the nature of the effects of advertising on the demand function of a monopolistically competitive firm in a fashion which leads to meaningful and testable hypotheses'.[28] Hadar and Hillinger [29] also set out to demonstrate that one can construct a meaningful and non-empty theory of monopolistic competition without the assumption of perfect knowledge. Hawkins, while accepting that the model of monopolistic competition needs modifying and developing, disagrees strongly with Cohen and Cyert in that he believes that 'there can be little doubt that the types of market conditions that Chamberlin and Robinson analysed are prevalent in practice'.[30] This viewpoint is shared by Lipsey [31] who argues that 'whatever the detractors of the theory may say, it seems that the model of a downward-sloping demand curve resulting from product differentiation, with the additional condition of freedom of entry, is a very useful one for the economist to have in his tool kit, because he will sometimes encounter industries that do come close to fulfilling these two conditions'. As Lipsey also points out, however, it is difficult to get the two sides in this debate to agree upon a fair test of the theory, so that the value of the model of monopolistic competition must for the time being remain indeterminate.

Chapter 6

The Theory of Oligopoly

Introduction

We have argued in the course of the preceding sections that neither the model of perfect competition nor that of monopoly reflects adequately the reality of present-day industrial organisation. In practice most industries appear currently to be characterised by competitive behaviour which typically reflects elements of both models. We have also seen that the model of monopolistic competition provided a worthy attempt to trace out a middle path, but that it also foundered largely on the basis of the unreality of its assumptions.

During the post-war period many attempts have been made to fill the void left by the decline from favour of the traditional theory of the firm, the bulk of which are now lumped together generically as 'the theory of oligopoly'. Although the many models which together form the theory of oligopoly often have their origins in ideas first postulated during the nineteenth century (as will be apparent from our discussion of duopoly models below), the stimulus for their further development was provided by the vast amount of empirical data uncovered by research conducted during and after the 1930s.

Unlike the theories of perfect competition and monopoly the theory of oligopoly has nothing specific to say about the number of firms within the industry. What matters instead is that changes in the behaviour of any one firm within the industry should subsequently cause a competitive reaction to take place, which in turn forces the original firm to modify its own behaviour. This interaction of behaviour among oligopolistic firms stems in large part from the uncertainty of the environment within which an oligopolistic firm operates. A monopolist, you will remember, controls his industry, and hence is able to predict in advance the most likely effects of any change in his policies. The perfectly competitive firm is largely passive in its operations but has the compensation of perfect knowledge of all market variables. The oligopolist, on the other hand, can never be sure about what will happen in the future, although the extent of his knowledge is likely, as we shall see, to be directly linked to the degree of inter-firm collusion within the industry. The nub of the problem facing each oligopolist is thus that he must always allow for competitive reactions to any policy change which he sets in motion, and these tend often to be unpredictable.[1]

There are three basic ways in which economists have attempted to construct a general theory of oligopoly:

(i) They have adapted the approach already employed for the development of the traditional models of the firm, which was to construct a theoretical model based upon a pre-determined set of assumptions; to produce hypotheses about firms' behaviour on the basis of these assumptions; and finally to verify or negate these hypotheses by reference to the relevant empirical data.

(ii) They have formulated a series of hypotheses about firms' behaviour based upon pre-existing empirical data, each of which relates to a fairly narrowly defined situation in which a firm might find itself. Whenever an empirically verifiable hypothesis is developed in this way it is added to all others previously verified in like manner. In this way it is hoped that it will eventually be possible to predict how a firm is likely to react in every conceivable situation.

(iii) They have developed what is known as the 'theory of games'. This constitutes various attempts to apply mathematical analysis to the oligopoly problem in order to develop a set of precepts concerning rational behaviour which, if followed by all the firms within an industry, will greatly reduce the uncertainty surrounding their future operations.

Chapter 7

Theoretical Models of Oligopolistic Behaviour

(i) *The Cournot Model*

The origins of theoretical models of oligopolistic behaviour date back to the appearance of simplified models of duopoly during the mid-nineteenth century. The best-known of such models was developed by Cournot [1] who discusses a situation of rivalry between two proprietors of mineral springs each selling identical bottles of spring water. Cournot assumes for simplicity that there are no costs of production, and also that no additional sellers of spring water are permitted by the local authorities to set themselves up in competition.

In the Cournot model each proprietor assumes that his rival will not alter his selling strategy provided that the latter remains able to dispose of his existing level of output. Hence each proprietor sets out to vary his pricing policy in such a way as to maximise his profits *while leaving his rivals' sales unaltered*. The fact, however, that both proprietors are selling an identical product implies that each must be charging the same price, for if this were not true then the cheaper product would corner the entire market whereas the expensive product would be unsaleable. The Cournot model thus explores the possible existence of a price which will simultaneously satisfy both proprietors, the solution being arrived at as follows.

We assume for simplicity that the demand curve for spring water may be represented geometrically as a straight line such as is depicted in Figure 7.1. Since quantity demanded at zero price is equal to 900 bottles, and since also the highest price which any potential consumer is willing to pay is thirty pence, the demand curve can also be represented algebraically by the equation $Q=900-30P$, where Q is the quantity sold and P is the price.

Now if we further assume that proprietor B is selling some output level q_2 which proprietor A must leave unaltered when selecting his optimal price–output combination in accordance with our above assumptions, the total output which proprietor A is potentially able to sell at various prices is given by total sales (Q) less B's sales (q_2) at each price, which can be expressed as $(Q-q_2)$. Proprietor A's demand curve, which is also his average-revenue curve, can thus be obtained by subtracting an output q_2 from market demand at all prices, thus yielding the straight line AA in Figure 7.1.

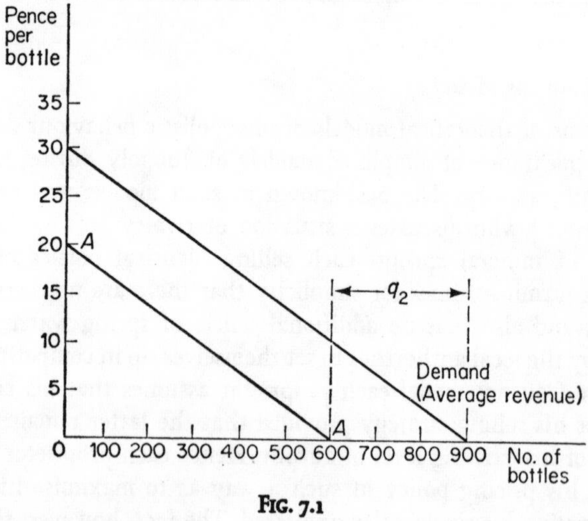

FIG. 7.1

Proprietor A maximises his profits where marginal cost is equal to marginal revenue in the customary way. Proprietor A's marginal-revenue curve bisects the horizontal axis midway to the point at which its corresponding average-revenue curve crosses that axis, which is at an output of $(900- q_2)$. Hence A's marginal-revenue curve bisects the axis at an output of $\frac{1}{2}(900-q_2)$. This is, of necessity, A's profit-maximising output because, in the absence of any production costs, marginal cost is by definition equal to zero at all times, and marginal revenue is itself equal to zero where it bisects the horizontal axis.

Now no matter what output level is initially chosen by proprietor B we can determine A's profit-maximising output, which we shall refer to below as q_1, by solving the equation $q_1=\frac{1}{2}(900-q_2)$ given the chosen value for q_2. Furthermore, we can plot geometrically all corresponding values for q_1 and q_2, as is illustrated in Figure 7.2, by solving the equation $q_1=\frac{1}{2}(900-q_2)$ for all possible values of q_2 ranging from 0 to 900. This yields a linear relationship which we denote as A's *reaction function*, since it shows how proprietor A will react to various output levels chosen by proprietor B.

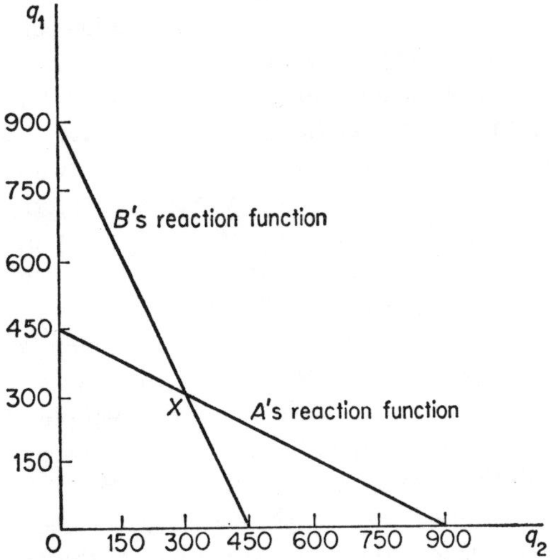

FIG. 7.2

It is evident that we can equally well derive a reaction function for proprietor B which illustrates how B will react to various output levels chosen by proprietor A. This can be represented by the functional relationship $q_2=\frac{1}{2}(900-q_1)$, and it appears as B's reaction function in Figure 7.2.

An equilibrium position is attained at the intersection of the two reaction functions, denoted by point X in Figure 7.2, since at point X the profit-minimising output chosen by each proprietor is compatible with the assumption that it must leave his rival's output unaltered. The output level corresponding to point X is found by solving the simultaneous equations which represent the reaction functions. Thus we have

$$q_1 = \tfrac{1}{2}(900 - q_2) \quad \text{or } q_1 + \tfrac{1}{2}q_2 = 450$$
$$q_2 = \tfrac{1}{2}(900 - q_1) \quad\quad q_2 + \tfrac{1}{2}q_1 = 450,$$

and this yields a value for both q_1 and q_2 of 300 bottles. Thus total sales by both proprietors amount to 600 bottles. This allows us to calculate the price per bottle by substitution into the demand curve formula $Q = 900 - 30P$ where Q is now equal to 600. Price per bottle is therefore equal to 10 pence and each proprietor earns a total revenue of £30. Since there are no costs of production, revenues and profits are the same thing, and each proprietor earns a profit of £30.

It is a fairly easy matter to alter the assumptions of the Cournot model in order to accommodate the need for one duopolist to leave unchanged by his own actions not his rival's sales but, for example, his rival's market share or profits. In every case, however, it seems at best illogical to expect an industry dominated by only two large firms to act competitively. It is more realistic to expect some form of collusion to take place, particularly collusion for the express purpose of maximising the joint profits of the two firms. In other words, we might reasonably expect the firms in question to act as if they were a monopoly, and to choose their price–output combination accordingly. We can apply this possibility to our basic model above by noting that the demand, or average-revenue, curve facing the two proprietors acting in collusion is now represented by the equation $Q = 900 - 30P$ since, between them, they are serving the entire market. Profits are maximised where marginal cost equals marginal revenue, which must occur where the marginal-revenue curve bisects the horizontal axis since marginal cost is equal to zero at all outputs. Since the marginal-revenue curve bisects the horizontal axis midway to the point at which that axis is bisected by the corresponding average-revenue curve, the joint profit-maximising output is thus equal to 450 bottles, and the price per bottle is found by solving the equation $450 = 900 - 300P$. Price is therefore equal to 15 pence per bottle. Total revenue and hence profit is equal to £67·50 which yields a profits of £33·75 to each proprietor. This profit exceeds by £3·75 the profit which each proprietor was able to earn while acting independently, and thus clearly demonstrates the benefits of collusion.

(ii) *The Stackelberg Model*

An alternative duopoly model was developed by von Stackelberg.[2] In this model each firm must choose whether to be a leader or a follower, where a leader is a firm which chooses its optimal price–output combination on the basis that the rival firm will take the leader's output as given, and where a follower is a firm which treats the rival firm's output as given and chooses its optimal price–output combination on that basis. Three possible combinations of leader and follower can be met. The first possibility is that one firm chooses to be a leader whereas the rival firm chooses to be a follower, and this allows us to develop a simple model with a stable equilibrium solution. A second possibility is that both firms choose to be followers, in which case the result is exactly the same as in the Cournot model since each firm acts in the expectation that the rival firm's output will remain unchanged. Hence this model also has a stable equilibrium solution.

Should, however, both firms wish to be leaders then no stable equilibrium is possible either until such time as one firm agrees to undertake the role of follower or until the two firms collude in order to maximise their joint profits. Where both firms wish to be leaders the situation is akin to that of economic warfare since each firm will be trying to force the rival firm into a subordinate role.

Von Stackelberg suggested that each firm calculates in advance the profits associated with the various leader–follower combinations open to it. Not surprisingly each firm tends to associate its greatest potential profit level with the situation in which it plays the role of leader while the rival firm plays the role of follower. But if the rival firm has itself come to the same conclusion both firms are more likely than not to choose the role of leader. Inevitably, however, the leader–leader combination is the least profitable for both firms, and is significantly inferior to the follower–follower combination in the absence of collusion. However, provided that the two firms are capable of learning from experience, we should expect the leader–leader combination to be quickly replaced by some other, more profitable, combination of strategies.

(iii) *The Kinked Demand Curve Model*

The main drawback to traditional duopoly models such as have been discussed above is their inherent lack of realism. There are so many possible assumptions which can be made to yield determinat solutions that we have no real way of choosing between them in the absence of substantial empirical data. There are, anyway, relatively few industries which resemble at all closely the classic duopoly structure, and for these reasons attention has turned during the twentieth century to exploring models of oligopoly for which the precise number of firms within an industry is by no means the main determinant in the search for a stable equilibrium solution.

A wide range of theoretical models of oligopoly is in existence, of which the best known is the kinked demand curve model which has its origins in two articles by Hall and Hitch [3] and Sweezy [4] respectively. This model is an attempt to provide a theoretical justification for the observed stickiness of price in highly concentrated oligopolistic industries during the Depression, and is conveniently summarised by Figure 7.3.

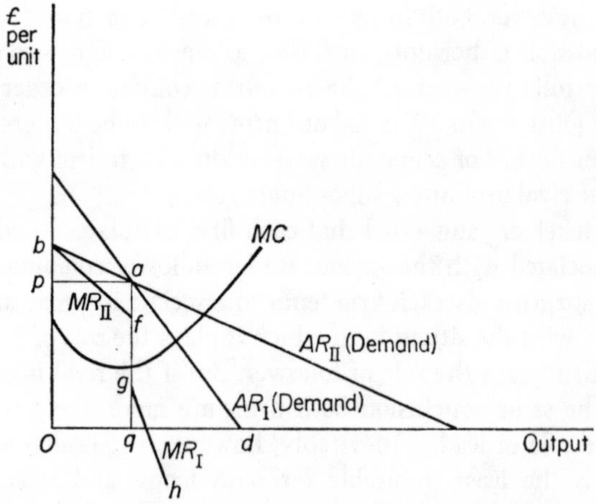

FIG. 7.3

In the diagram we have drawn two demand (average-revenue) curves crossing at point *a*, and we are seeking to analyse why we might expect price to be sticky at a level of *Op* for every firm, where *Op* is the prevailing price for all firms within the industry at a particular point in time. Demand curve I relates to the situation in which any rise or fall in the price charged by one firm induces all other firms to follow suit, whereas demand curve II relates to the situation in which any rise or fall in the price charged by one firm is ignored by all other firms.

We begin by considering what will happen should one individual firm decide to raise its selling price above the prevailing level of *Op*. Such a move will make the firm's product relatively expensive as compared to all of its rivals' products. Hence we would expect price-conscious customers to quickly transfer their custom to other, relatively less-expensive, firms, with the net result that the firm which raised its price will suffer a substantial loss of sales. This is reflected by a movement along the section *ab* of demand curve II where the curve is highly elastic. As a consequence this strategy will not be considered worthwhile by any single firm because the reduction in sales will also imply a drop in profits, particularly where average cost rises as output falls.

But suppose that a single firm decides to lower its price. It will then become the only cheap producer within the industry and, were its rivals to ignore its behaviour, the net result would be that a large number of its rivals' customers would transfer their custom to the relatively cheap producer. It is, however, most unlikely that the price-cutter's rivals will turn a blind eye to this strategy which will have the effect initially of reducing their profits. Hence we must logically expect price-cutting to be competitive, probably with all firms eventually lowering their prices to the same extent. Where, however, all firms simultaneously cut their prices there is unlikely to be a major expansion of total sales of the product unless it is, for example, something particularly desirable which had previously been too highly priced to sell extensively as a mass-produced commodity. But if price falls noticeably whereas output barely increases, as illustrated by a movement down the section *ad* of demand curve I above, each firm will suffer both a substantial loss of revenue and also, unless the economies of scale are sufficient to compensate, a corresponding loss of profit. This applies both to the original price-cutter as well as to his rivals, so that no individual firm will regard it as a profitable strategy to pursue.

Now in the course of the above analysis we have discussed movements along a kinked demand curve *b*, *a*, *d* – hence the name of this theory. As we have suggested the precise implications in terms of profit gains or losses associated with each strategy depend both upon the shape of the respective demand curves and also upon the shape of the firm's average-cost curve, since falls in output will normally be accompanied by rising average cost and increased output by falling average cost. It is of particular importance to note that the firm's marginal-revenue curve, corresponding to the kinked average-revenue curve *bad*, is discontinuous, with section *bf* corresponding to section *ba* of demand curve II, and section *gh* corresponding to section *ad* on demand curve I. The marginal-revenue curve is thus represented by the line *bfgh*. Now if, as illustrated in Figure 7.3, the firm's marginal-cost curve passes through the vertical section *fg* of the marginal-revenue curve the firm has no incentive to alter the prevailing price of *Op*, since even if the marginal-cost curve shifts upwards over time the firm's profit-maximising output, defined by the intersection of the two curves, remains unaltered, in which case the optimal price-output combination itself remains unchanged.

It is apparent, however, that the above analysis has ready applicability to only the depression phase of the trade cycle, since it is during such a time that economising consumers respond to increased prices by switching from one supplier to another. Furthermore, a general price cut may do little in a depression to stimulate additional sales.

The model is less satisfactory under boom conditions. When consumers have money to spare, and are competing for available supplies of goods, a price rise by one individual firm may provide an open invitation for rival firms to follow suit, secure in the knowledge that if all firms raise their prices simultaneously each one individually will lose very few would-be customers. In other words, demand is considerably less elastic in response to a price rise than under depressed conditions. In prosperous times prices tend to rise regularly, generally accompanied by the excuse, truthful or otherwise, that costs have risen. Where this happens, however, the logic of the kinked demand curve model is contradicted.

As with any theory it is necessary to compare the prediction, that is of sticky prices, against the available evidence, such as it is. We find that between 1926 and 1938 prices remained virtually unchanged in the U.S. sulphur industry, an unusually long period of price stability. Also in 1934 in the U.S. potash industry one major firm raised its price without its rivals following suit, with the result that the firm's sales fell off dramatically. As a result it subsequently cut its prices to below the level prevailing in the rest of the industry, to which all of its rivals responded by lowering their own prices by an equivalent amount.[5] But in 1947 when Stigler investigated seven major U.S.

oligopolies[6] he found that in no case did the above theory accurately portray the way in which these oligopolies were found to operate, and a follow-up study by Simon[7] of business magazine advertising rates in the United States between 1955 and 1964 also failed to lend empirical support to the kinked demand curve hypothesis.

Unfortunately both studies were subject to certain drawbacks which may have biased the results.[8] It was in order to overcome these drawbacks that Primeaux and Bomball compared municipally owned and privately owned electric utilities in the United States during the periods 1959–62 and 1964–70. Their study, along with Simon's, set out to re-examine Stigler's assertion that 'the kinky demand curve would prove to be an incorrect or unimportant construction if oligopoly prices were as flexible as monopoly and/or competitive prices'. They examined price changes in time-series data for each firm operating in cities with two electric-utility firms and for municipally owned monopoly utility firms. They found firstly that there was 'significantly more price rigidity in the monopoly market structure than in the oligopoly market structure';[9] secondly that 'price decreases were not followed any more frequently than price increases';[10] and thirdly that 'price increases were more nearly simultaneous than were price decreases'.[11] Since all of these findings expressly contradict the assumptions of the kinked demand curve model the evidence closely supports the conclusions of both Stigler and Simon. By way of final conclusion they note that 'perhaps the behaviour observed in price wars, which do tend to support the assumptions of the theory, merely reflect temporary disequilibrium conditions in imperfectly competitive markets, and may not apply to a general case of oligopoly conduct'.[12]

Thus the theory does not appear to have any general validity[13] although it may reflect reality where inter-firm knowledge is poor,[14] for example in a new industry or where new firms enter an established industry, since they will not, under such circumstances, have any knowledge of likely competitive reactions to variations in price. But even in these limited cases the firms may quickly learn that they are better off with collusion.

(iv) *Dominant-Firm Price Leadership*

We have already suggested in the kinked demand curve model above that under certain circumstances one firm within an industry may decide to change its price with all of its rivals following suit after a short time lag. Several models have been developed to explore the outcome of this kind of price leadership and these are customarily grouped into three categories the first of which, known as dominant-firm price leadership, describes a situation in which one firm is so large relative to other firms within an industry that it is able to subjugate their pricing policy to its own. (This is unlike the situation which applies in collusive price leadership as discussed below, each seller acting individually in his own best interests but with only one seller having the power to influence prices.)

The underlying principle of the dominant-firm model is that the dominant firm derives its demand curve by subtracting from the industry demand curve the sales which all the other firms within the industry would want to make at each price level which the dominant firm might conceivably set. Given this assumption, and also an accurate estimate of both its own and other firms' marginal-cost curves, the dominant firm can readily select that price which will maximise its profits, as depicted in Figure 7.4.

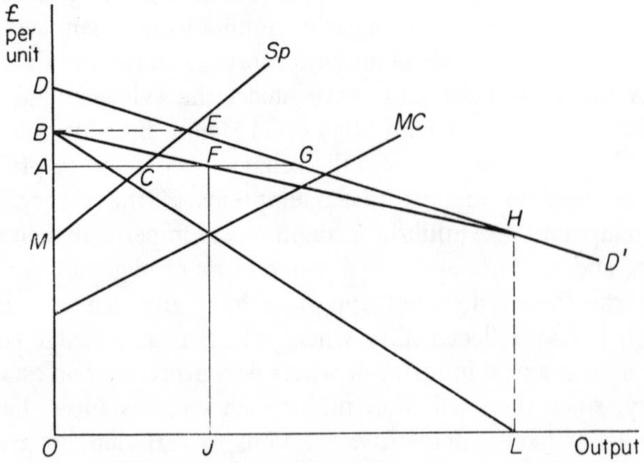

FIG. 7.4

In Figure 7.4 *DD'* is the market demand curve, MC is the dominant firm's marginal-cost curve, and *Sp* is the marginal-cost (supply) curve of all other firms within the industry. Now at price OB the minor firms will want to supply the entire market, and this will also apply for all prices greater than OB given our assumption that the minor firms are allowed to sell all they wish at the price selected by the dominant firm. The dominant firm thus makes no sales unless price is less than *OB*, which implies that its demand curve commences at point B itself. At a price of OA the minor firms will want to supply a quantity *AC*, leaving the dominant firm free to supply CG units. This yields a point F on its demand curve such that CG=AF.

By following the same procedure for all possible prices we determine the dominant firm's demand curve to be *BFHD′*, where the section *HD′* lies on the market demand curve because the minor firms will not wish to sell anything at prices below OM. The marginal-revenue curve corresponding to section *BH* of the dominant firm's demand curve is given by *BL*, and the dominant firm's profit-maximising output is found to be *OJ* units which is the output at which its *MC* and *MR* curves intersect. The chosen selling price is therefore OA, at which price the minor firms will sell AC units and the dominant firm AF units, which when added together amount to the total market demand AG at a price of OA.

A fair amount of empirical evidence exists to support the hypothesis of dominant-firm price leadership,[15] although the model has elsewhere been treated with not much short of contempt.[16] The complaint most often voiced is that the model over-simplifies inter-firm price relationships [17] but it is also pointed out that a firm whose dominance is vulnerable in the longer term because of anticipated expansion by existing rivals and the entry of new rivals into its industry, may well do better for itself by opting for a higher price and higher profits in the short term even at the cost of a more rapid decline in its market share over time.[18]

(v) *Barometric Price Leadership*

Barometric price leadership describes a situation in which one particular firm is more often than not the first to announce changes in price. In contrast with the model previously discussed, however, the price leader in this case does not have to be either the dominant or the largest firm within the industry. Indeed the absolute size of the price leader is of itself inconsequential,[19] the important criterion being whether or not the price leader is adept at selecting a price which will prove acceptable to other firms within the industry. The price leader thus acts as a barometer faithfully representing the wishes of most firms within the industry, and if the existing price leader fails at any time to act as a barometer for the other firms then its role as price leader will be taken over by another firm.

There is not, however, much evidence which serves to distinguish clearly this type of price leadership from those others under discussion. In his articles Stigler [20] used the term barometric price leadership to apply to all industries where there was no dominant firm, and justified this largely by reference to a lengthy quotation by a spokesman for Standard Oil of Ohio. Markham,[21] however, was at pains to point out the distinction between competitive and collusive barometric price leadership, and Bain [22] was very scathing about evidence which purported to demonstrate the existence of price leadership of the former kind. Better-known studies containing references to barometric price leadership, such as that by Kaplan, Dirlam and Lanzillotti,[23] can more appropriately be regarded as providing evidence of informal collusive price leadership, to which we turn our attention below.[24]

(vi) *Informal Collusive Price Leadership*

According to Markham [25] there may be circumstances in which all the firms within an industry choose to follow the price set by one amongst their number in order to ensure that they are acting more or less in concert rather than competing so fiercely as to cause widespread hardship. This stems from a realisation that they will be much better off, on average, as a result of replacing competition by co-operation. At the same time the co-operation is not explicit and overt, which would in all probability be against the law, but stems from confidence that rival firms will adopt the same policy.

Provided that the price leader is reasonably adept at estimating what is best for the industry as a whole, it is possible for the industry to approach its joint profit-maximising price and output. This is a relatively simple matter if we adopt Markham's own assumptions: few sellers; restricted entry; homogeneous products; similar cost curves; and unresponsive demand when price is cut. However, these assumptions are unreasonably restrictive and in practice can be treated only as a special case.[26] If, for example, we make allowances for the possibility that the colluding firms have varying levels of average cost, then it becomes much more difficult for the price leader to hit upon a price which is satisfactory to all concerned, and the problems faced by the price leader will not differ markedly from those faced by a dominant firm such as were discussed above.

(vii) *Formal Collusive Price Leadership*

Although formal collusive price leadership is illegal unless it has been given the blessing of the Restrictive Trade Practices Court, cases doubtless exist today, and certainly did before the passing of the Restrictive Trade Practices Act in 1956, of firms which formally get together for the express purpose of determining their joint profit-maximising price and output.

The enforcement of cartel agreements is, however, fraught with difficulties. First, it is necessary that the combined output of all the producers be restricted to an amount which will maximise profits at the agreed price. This is, however, unlikely to occur unless each member of the cartel is assigned a production quota which it is not allowed to exceed. The allocation of production quotas must itself be linked to the relative efficiency of each firm, since the group as a whole cannot maximise its profits unless the cheapest producers are assigned larger quotas than the relatively expensive producers. But this arrangement is unlikely to be to the tastes of the inefficient firms who may prefer to break up the cartel rather than be forced to curtail output. Alternatively, they may force the other firms to adopt a less profitable set of production quotas.

A further substantial difficulty is that each member of the cartel may come to the conclusion that it is more profitable to cheat by either altering its price or output or both together, provided of course that the other firms are expected to continue to adhere to the agreed price and quotas. Some means of detecting those who cheat is therefore called for,[27] and if a reasonably foolproof method can be developed, the incidence of cheating will be drastically reduced. This is because a firm which sets out to cheat will know that its rivals will find out and subsequently retaliate, in which event the profits earned by each firm will be less than those available where the firms adhere to the cartel agreement.

Empirical evidence about cartel agreements is hard to come by, in part because the illegality of such agreements promotes an attitude of secrecy,[28] and it is, anyway, difficult to assess the effectiveness of a cartel since we have no real way of estimating what would have happened in the absence of collusion. We would, however, expect cartels to flourish in the absence of stringent controls since it is fairly easy to demonstrate that it is, in general, more profitable for a firm to collude than to pursue an independent line.

(viii) *Parallel Pricing in Practice*

We have already referred in passing to various studies which purport to provide empirical evidence with respect to price leadership. In addition an attempt was made to clarify the meaning and effects of price leadership in the United Kingdom, commencing in May 1971, which culminated in the publication of the Monopolies Commission's *Report* on parallel pricing.[29]

For the purposes of the *Report* parallel pricing was defined as [30] the practice by which two or more sellers in an oligopolistic market, when changing their prices, do so together, by similar amounts or proportions, and having regard to the interests of the group of sellers as a whole'. The *Report* then goes on to distinguish the various kinds of price leadership as enumerated above. When discussing collusive price leadership the important point is made that [31] 'Uniformity of list or published prices may, however, conceal variations between sellers in such matters as discounts, transport and credit charges and the like. In many industries the real price of the product is not just the list price, and sellers may welcome the opportunity for independent action on discounts, and so on, even though they follow a co-ordinated policy with respect to list prices, particularly in times of excess capacity.' [32]

The greatest controversy, however, concerns the alleged uniformity between barometric price leadership and pricing in competitive conditions. It is argued that barometric price leadership is highly responsive to market conditions and that it is a 'symptom of the existence of effective competition which makes it impossible to sustain the more disciplined type of leadership'.[33] The Monopolies Commission, however, took the view that no form of price leadership would correspond to competitive competitions, although they accepted that barometric price leadership was less harmful to the public than the stronger forms of parallel pricing. 'However oligopolists choose to co-ordinate their behaviour, the result is likely to be a level of prices and profits higher than would prevail with a large number of sellers, and a price structure more rigid in the face of changing cost and demand conditions.'[34]

But if price leadership, whatever form it takes, is to be regarded as harmful, then there is an implicit assumption that price leadership is itself the cause of the harm. This conclusion is not, however, acceptable to those[35] who believe that barometric leadership and competitive conditions are compatible with one another. Indeed the Polanyis go so far as to argue[36] that by drawing the conclusion[37] that 'parallel pricing may have certain particular detriments commonly associated with the exercise of market power'[38] the Monopolies Commission itself effectively admitted that the harm done in conditions of parallel pricing, in terms of prices and costs exceeding the competitive level, is due not to the parallel pricing itself but to the existence of monopolistic conditions which enable the more disciplined type of leadership to prevail.

The Monopolies Commission reached a number of conclusions in their *Report*. First, although they considered the empirical evidence to be 'unsystematic and not wholly reliable' they concluded that parallel pricing was 'a fairly widespread phenomenon over industry as a whole'.[39] In all the industries covered by the *Report* (which excluded consideration of dominant-firm price leadership) the usual price leader was the seller with the largest share of the market,[40] although it was not clear whether this was the most efficient seller. The Commission felt that competition in other than published prices might weaken the cohesiveness of any group of sellers practising parallel pricing, as might 'differences in sellers' levels of costs, market shares, expectations about future growth prospects or simply managerial styles and aspirations'.[41] As a result, the price leader might not always be followed by other sellers, especially where the seller is neither the largest nor the most efficient producer, and 'where there is therefore great uncertainty among the group as to the appropriate action each should take on the occasion of any price change'.[42]

The *Report* also set out the conditions which would help promote highly disciplined parallel pricing. These were where a group of sellers produced a relatively standardised product; operated in a highly concentrated industry; was protected by entry and other barriers against new and overseas competition; had limited opportunities for concealed competition in discounts and other variations from published prices;[43] where demand for the output of the industry as a whole was relatively insensitive to changes in the general level of prices;[44] and where there was an absence of frequent changes in products and production methods resulting from technical progressiveness.[45] To this the Polanyis responded by suggesting that one had only to examine the five industries studied in the *Report* to deduce that 'there are indeed few industries which meet these specifications (particularly on a lasting basis) and that if they do they must have strong monopoly conditions quite apart from the existence of parallel pricing'.[46]

The final concern of the *Report* was to discuss the consequences of parallel pricing as far as efficiency and costs were concerned. These the Commission considered to be 'an excessive level of advertising and similar non-production costs'; a retardation of the process whereby 'the more efficient sellers are able to expand their share of the market'; and a reduction of pressure on all sellers 'including those with the lowest costs, to maintain the highest degree of efficiency'.[47] These assertions are disputed by the Polanyis, who themselves conclude that[48]

Since most price leadership is of the barometric type, and in these cases it results in avoidance of inflexibility of prices and thereby creates conditions where prices and costs are likely to be similar to what would emerge in independent competition between many suppliers, it follows that the outcome will often be 'positively beneficial'. In achieving prices and costs no higher than the 'competitive norm', it is not the method but the result which matters.

Chapter 8

Generalising from Hypotheses about Observed Behaviour

Relatively little attention has been paid to this approach to the oligopoly problem, perhaps because it cannot be expected to yield many insights into oligopolistic behaviour until much more empirical information has been gathered together. A useful summary of progress in this direction appears in Lipsey,[1] who selects as his central hypothesis that of *qualified joint profit maximisation*.[2] He defines this as follows:[3]

Firms that recognise that they are in rivalry with one another will be motivated by two opposing forces; one moves them towards policies that maximise the combined profits of the existing group of sellers, the other moves them away from the joint profit-maximising position. Both forces are associated with observable characteristics of firms, markets and products, and thus we can make predictions about market behaviour on the basis of these characteristics.

This hypothesis explicitly allows for the fact that the actions of the rivals will affect the size of the pie as well as its division amongst them. This reflects the fact that the group of sellers must operate in the context of a downward-sloping demand curve, and the total revenue earned by the group hence varies in response to variations in the group's collective pricing policy (the only exception being where the elasticity of demand is equal to unity). If the rivals behave collectively they can operate just as a monopolist would, and they would adopt whichever policy will maximise their joint profits, whereas if all firms simultaneously pursue their own interests, joint profits will be greatly reduced. However, even if all the firms are agreed in principle upon collective action, it may pay *one single* firm to depart from the joint profit-maximising price if, by so doing, it can increase its profits. This in turn will depend upon the way in which its rivals react to its unilateral action, as the following example demonstrates.

Let the joint profit-maximising price yield total profits of £100 for a group of ten firms, each of which is allocated an equal share of total profit to the tune of £10 apiece. By lowering its selling price one firm subsequently obtains for itself 14½ per cent of the available market. Once, however, the other firms within the group discover that the price agreement has been broken they respond by lowering their own prices to the same extent as the original price-cutter. Consequently, the whole group moves away from its most profitable price–output combination and available profits fall to £84. The original price-cutter now earns 14½ per cent of £84 which is equal to £12, and has therefore improved its position. The other nine firms now each serve 9½ per cent of the market and therefore earn a profit of £8 apiece, which is less than before.

The above example thus illustrates one possible situation which is that in which a single firm profits at the expense of its rivals by deliberately undercutting the joint profit-maximising price. However, this will only hold good provided the price-cutter can retain its enlarged market share once the other firms have lowered their prices, and provided the available profits do not fall to such an extent that the enlarged share of the smaller total profit amounts to a lower level of profit than the price-cutter was originally earning.

Lipsey then goes on to enumerate eight hypotheses about behaviour in oligopolistic markets.[4] Of greatest significance is that relating to barriers to entry which many commentators have noted to be greater (*a*) the greater the economies of scale; (*b*) the greater the degree of product differentiation; and (*c*) the greater the level of brand-name advertising.

We may note first of all that to produce cheaply may require a large throughput, and this normally takes time for a new entrant to achieve since, for the most part, customers need to be attracted away from established producers. In general, new entrants can only hope to capture a small share of the market in the short term. In order to increase their market share they must obviously set their prices on a par with, or below, those of established rivals. But if scale economies are substantial the new entrant's costs will remain high relative to those of established producers until its sales have been expanded sufficiently to acquire the benefits of large-scale operation. Thus a new entrant must expect to make either minimal profits or even losses in the short term until its costs have been reduced to a level commensurate with those of its main competitors. However, the full benefits of scale can in many cases be obtained at relatively low levels of output (see pp. 86–90), and there is nothing in theory to prevent a new entrant from growing to an optimal size other than in those markets which can only be served by one firm of efficient size. Given this fact it is not surprising to discover that established firms use a wide range of devices in order to make life tougher for prospective entrants. Two devices in particular are in wide usage.

(1) We may note that if the product is one such that consumers switch brands with any frequency then an increase in the number of brands sold by existing firms will reduce the likelihood of sales to a new entrant. Where brand switching is common there will be a large floating population of brand switchers who constitute potential customers for a new firm. But a person switching brands is able to choose between both the products of a new entrant and also those of existing producers which he is not currently purchasing. Therefore, the greater the number of brands sold by existing firms the more diffused will be the effect of brand switching, and the lower will be the percentage of all brand switchers gained by each single brand produced by the new entrant. Hence the proliferation of brands by established firms can be interpreted as a defensive reaction intended to make it more difficult for a new entrant to pick up brand switchers.

(2) We may also note that if there is a substantial amount of brand-name advertising then a new entrant will have to spend a great deal on advertising its products in order to bring them to the public's attention. Where, however, the new entrant's sales are relatively small this implies that advertising cost per unit sold will be very heavy relative to that of an established competitor.

The above two factors suggest an explanation for a phenomenon associated particularly with industries such as tobacco products and detergents which are characterised by a small number of very large producers. In such industries established firms tend to produce a wide range of similar products each of which is advertised heavily, with the emphasis being placed upon the brand name rather than upon the name of the parent company. This largely results from the fact that technological barriers to entry are weak in these industries and economies of scale are exhausted at output levels which are low relative to the size of the total available market. Hence market domination can only be retained via heavy advertising expenditures and brand proliferation.

Chapter 9

The Theory of Games[1]

(i) *Introduction*

We have already noted that when a firm is planning its future strategy it must make allowances for the response of its competitors to any action which it takes. A strategy must therefore include not merely a set of opening moves but also further sets of counter moves which can be brought into play in order to redirect the firm towards the attainment of its original objectives after competitors have responded to its opening gambit. It is evident however that a similar line of reasoning can also be applied to each of its competitors since each of them in turn will need to develop a strategy which makes allowances for various alternative opening and counter moves by all other firms within the market.

It would appear likely on the face of it that the process of move and counter move will be a never-ending one, with no one firm ever being able to fully achieve its objectives. In practice, however, there is invariably some solution which, although it does not permit of any firm achieving all of its objectives, is acceptable to all parties simultaneously because it is deemed by all to be preferable to the continuance of a conflict situation.

The problem of conflict of interest is, for each competitor, a problem of individual decision-making under conditions of risk and uncertainty.

Risk accompanies a decision where each alternative course of action produces one of a limited number of pay-offs, and where the probability of occurrence of each possible pay-off is known. *Uncertainty* accompanies a decision where each alternative course of action produces one of a limited number of pay-offs, but where the probability of occurrence of each possible pay-off cannot be meaningfully assessed.

Game theory is an attempt to postulate precepts of strategy which, if followed by the participants in a competitive situation, will enable them to reduce the degree of uncertainty surrounding their actions. This is not accomplished directly by assuming knowledge of what an opponent will do, but indirectly by assuming that the opponent has certain information and that he is motivated in certain ways, or, in other words, that he behaves rationally.

More specifically a game is defined as follows. A *game* is a decision situation involving conflict of interest between two or more interacting decision-makers in which the following conditions hold:

(1) each decision-maker has available to him a set of two or more well-specified choices or sequences of choices called *plays*;
(2) every possible combination of plays available to the players leads to a well-defined end state (win, lose or draw) which terminates the game; and
(3) a specified pay-off for each player is associated with each end state.

These conditions can most easily be represented in the form of a pay-off matrix, the entries of which constitute the pay-off associated with each possible combination of choices by the players. We will restrict ourselves below to examples in which there are either two players or combinations of players.

		Player *B*'s possible plays				
		b_1	b_2	b_3	b_4	b_n
Player *A*'s possible plays	a_1	x_{11}	x_{12}	x_{13}	x_{14}	x_{1n}
	a_2	x_{21}	x_{22}	x_{23}	x_{24}	x_{2n}
	a_3	x_{31}	x_{32}	x_{33}	x_{34}	x_{3n}
	a_4	x_{41}	x_{42}	x_{43}	x_{44}	x_{4n}
	.	.	.	.	.	.
	.	.	.	.	.	.
	.	.	.	.	.	.
	a_n	x_{n1}	x_{n2}	x_{n3}	x_{n4}	x_{nn}

Now where each player knows the value of the pay-offs in the matrix, and also that his competitors are aware of the strategic principles (as set out below) underlying competitive behaviour, his pursuit of a rational objective can effectively be undertaken under conditions of certainty about the outcome of his strategy.

The preceding paragraph can best be clarified by setting out some illustrative examples of competitive games.

(ii) *Two-Person Zero-Sum Games*

Let us begin by considering a two-person game (duopoly) in which whatever one player gains the other loses and vice versa. This is called a *two-person zero-sum game.* In the matrix shown here the pay-offs are gains to player A and losses to player B.

		Player *B* (losses)	
		b_1	b_2
Player *A* (gains)	a_1	3	9
	a_2	5	7

Now if A knows that B will choose b_1 he should select a_2 rather than a_1 for a total gain of 5. If, on the other hand, he knows that B will chose b_2 he should choose a_1 rather than a_2 for a gain of 9.

But which choice of strategy will be made by B? A should reason as follows: 'B will observe that if he selects b_1 the most that he can lose is 5, whereas the greatest loss which he can sustain through choosing b_2 is 9. B will therefore opt for strategy b_1 and from this I conclude that my optimum choice of strategy is a_2.' This line of reasoning is based upon the *minimax* principle which suggests that the loser should act so as to *minimise his maximum possible loss*, which is the same thing as minimising the winner's maximum possible gain.

At the same time B should attempt to assess rationally which choice of strategy will be made by A before deciding which strategy to adopt himself. B should reason as follows: 'A will observe that if he selects a_1 the least that he can gain is 3, whereas if he selects a_2 his minimum pay-off is 5. Therefore he will select a_2 and in response I should select b_1. This line of reasoning is based upon the *maximum* principle which suggests that the winner should act so as to *maximise his minimum possible gain.*

In the above game we thus find that both players selected the same strategy combination a_2b_1 as the most likely outcome of the game, and that each player chose the strategy anticipated by his opponent when the latter was formulating his own choice of strategy. An important aspect of this solution is that neither player is able to improve his pay-off *in the absence of a change in strategy by his opponent.* The solution therefore satisfies both players simultaneously, and neither is tempted to reconsider his choice of strategy.

A solution to a two-person zero-sum game is not, however, always provided by an entry in the pay-off matrix itself. Such a solution exists only if the pay-off matrix contains an entry which is the *highest in its column and the lowest in its row.* Such an entry is known as a *saddle point.* A pay-off matrix can conceivably contain more than one saddle point. On the other hand, it may have no saddle point at all, as is true of the pay-off matrix shown here.

		Player *B* (losses)	
		b_1	b_2
Player *A* (gains)	a_1	5	9
	a_2	7	3

B's choice of strategy based upon the minimax principle is b_1. A's choice of strategy based upon the maximin principle is a_1. The strategy combination a_1b_1, however, satisfies neither player. A will see the opportunity to improve his pay-off by switching to strategy a_2 in the hope that B will leave his strategy unchanged. On the other hand, B will respond to the strategy combination a_2b_1 by himself switching to b_2 in the hope that A will leave his strategy unchanged. But this will induce A to change his strategy once again to a_1, and so forth. Thus there is no equilibrium combination of strategies in the above matrix.

It is, however, a relatively simple matter to determine the equilibrium value of this type of matrix using, for example, the 'mixed strategies' technique.[2] Indeed it can be shown that any two-person zero-sum game, regardless of the number of strategies available to the two players, has a unique equilibrium value. Unfortunately this is the only part of game theory that is essentially complete.

Some of the reasons why game theory has not been found to be of greater usefulness in competitive-decision problems are as follows. First, in a real-life situation the number of competitors is often greater than two. This leads to significant difficulties for analytical purposes since as soon as three or more players are involved it becomes possible for coalitions of players to be formed. For example, in a game with three players, two may form a coalition against the third, and by agreeing upon their own selection of strategies they may be able to guarantee themselves pay-offs greater than those which would have resulted from three-way rivalry. Thus the situation can become too complex for useful analysis.[3]

Also, in the real world, situations are not usually of a zero-sum type whereby one competitor's gains are exactly offset by another's losses, and this makes it very difficult to set up a game in a form which is amenable to solution by standard mathematical techniques. For these reasons there are many commentators who believe that game theory has taught us virtually nothing that we did not know already.[4]

(iii) *The Prisoner's Dilemma*

Some interesting conclusions concerning the tendency of firms to collude can, however, be obtained by reference to a simple two-person *non*-constant-sum game. A non-constant-sum game requires that a pay-off matrix be set up for each player individually. An example of such a two-person game is illustrated in the matrix shown here. As can be seen one player's gains are no longer equal to the other player's losses. The total gain from any strategy combination is found by adding together the pay-offs to each individual player. Thus the pay-off for strategy A_1B_1 is 25.

A's pay-offs

	B_1	B_2	B_3
A_1	11	7	5
A_2	13	11	10
A_3	15	14	13

B's pay-offs

	A_1	A_2	A_3
B_1	14	12	8
B_2	17	14	9
B_3	19	17	12

Now we have already noted in the context of a constant-sum game that the criterion which should be adopted by a player expecting a positive pay-off is the maximin criterion. The application of this criterion indicates strategy choices of A_3 and B_3 respectively for a joint gain of 25, consisting of $A_3B_3=13$ and $B_3A_3=12$. This happens to be an equilibrium solution satisfactory to both parties because the chosen strategy combination identifies the saddle point in each matrix.

A_3B_3 is not, however, the joint profit-maximising strategy combination, since the strategy A_2B_3 yields a total gain of 27. Hence the players can improve upon the joint pay-off obtainable under competitive conditions by colluding in order to identify the joint profit-maximising strategy. It will however, be necessary for B to cede to A part of his improved profits (up from 12 to 17) because otherwise A will be disadvantaged by the collusion (down from 13 to 10). Hence it will be necessary for the players to agree upon a split of 14 to A and 13 to B if the collusion is to prove satisfactory to both players.

A variant of the above game is known as the *prisoner's dilemma*,[5] this name originating from the nature of the problem as set out below. Two known criminals are held by the police for questioning in connection with a bank robbery. The police are more or less certain of their guilt, but the identification of the thieves by witnesses proves inconclusive because the thieves wore stockings over their heads. The police do, however, have cast-iron proof that the criminals they have apprehended stole a car which the police believe was used by the thieves for their getaway.

		Accomplice	
		Denies charge	Queen's evidence
Criminal	Denies charge	3 months	10 years
	Queen's evidence	Freedom	5 years

The prisoners are separated by the police and put into individual cells from which they cannot communicate with each other. Each criminal is then invited to turn 'Queen's evidence' in return for which he is offered his freedom, whereas his accomplice, should he deny the charge, will get an especially heavy sentence. Each criminal already knows that if both accomplices deny the charge of robbery they will both be sentenced for stealing a vehicle.

The essence of the dilemma is that neither criminal knows whether his accomplice will admit or deny the major charge made against him. Each criminal must make his own choice in relation to the pay-offs shown in the matrix.

Now if each criminal believes that his accomplice can be trusted to deny the charge of robbery then it will pay him to turn Queen's evidence and go free. If, however, he does not trust his accomplice and expects the latter to admit the charge and turn Queen's evidence against him then it will still pay him to confess in order to halve his possible sentence. In fact it can be seen from Matrix 5 that the strategy of turning Queen's evidence dominates the strategy of denying the charge. Thus we would expect each criminal to admit the charge and for both to be sent down for five years. It is clear, however, that the optimal strategy is for each criminal to deny the charge and to be sent down for only three months, but in the absence of collusion this is unlikely to transpire.

(iv) *Experiments in Oligopolistic Situations*

A good deal of work has been done on the testing of hypotheses in oligopoly theory by utilising the type of approach analysed above in the context of the prisoner's dilemma game. An early study by Lave[6] employed repetitions of the prisoner's dilemma game itself with players who were prevented from communicating among themselves. He found that, given time to learn, some three-quarters of the players eventually adopted strategies which maximised their joint pay-off with other players, but that there was a strong tendency for players to engage in underhand behaviour on the final move of the game when further retaliation was ruled out.

Dolbear *et al.*[7] conducted a test on fairly similar lines in which students were used to represent firms which were not permitted to communicate with one another other than through alterations in prices. Firms were able to choose either from among two possible prices (the prisoner's dilemma matrix) or from among thirty different prices. Each game consisted of thirty-two trials of which the first five (learning) trials and the final (double-cross) trial were eliminated. In the case of the 2×2 matrix 63·6 per cent of the players arrived at the joint profit-maximising price at least once, and 27·3 per cent of the players stuck to that price once achieved, whereas the respective figures for the 30 × 30 matrix were 16·7 per cent in both cases. Of the twelve pairs of players who used the large matrix eight achieved varying levels of profit falling between the co-operative and non-co-operative maxima (defined as highest and lowest prices in the small matrix). This provided evidence that the large matrix offered alternative choices which varied with the degree of co-operation, but left unexplained the reasons for the failure of one-third of the pairs to settle within the expected price range.[8]

Dolbear *et al.*[9] also conducted some controlled experiments in order to explore further the conclusion drawn in an earlier study by Fouraker and Siegel [10] that a change in the market from duopoly to triopoly produced a decrease in the extent of collusion. Students who were employed to represent firms in these experiments were prevented from communicating with one another and were given varying amounts of information about their rivals' profits. Complete information was given in experiments with two- and four-firm markets, and incomplete information was given for two-, four- and sixteen-firm markets.

Their first finding was that the likelihood of firms colluding tacitly in order to maximise their joint profits rose noticeably in line with a steady fall in the number of firms within the industry.[11] They also considered to what extent variations in the availability of information would affect the ability of firms to reach tacit agreement. Each player was allowed fifteen trials of which the first seven and final three were excluded in order to remove all sources of bias.[12] They found that profit per player was higher with complete information in the two-firm market, but marginally lower in the four-firm market. No comparisons for the sixteen-firm market were possible. In general they concluded that collusion became easier as information improved, but in view of the small sample sizes employed they also advised that the 'results must be viewed as suggestive rather than as conclusive'.[13]

Collusion is also likely to be affected by prior experience of price wars. Murphy,[14] for example, conducted an experiment to test the hypothesis that 'the fear and threat of losses may be the decisive factor in real bargaining which forces sellers not to undercut their competitors to a zero profit price'. He based his experiment on the

Fouraker–Siegel experiments in which players were unable to communicate, utilising 18 pairs of players over a series of 24 trials. Unlike his predecessors, however, he changed the profit table to allow for losses at low-price bids. He concluded that 'The threat of losses encourages sellers to bicker in a price zone which allows profits. Eventually, perceptive sellers realise the advantages of co-operation and they seek to establish that common price which provides the optimal mutual maximisation of profits.'

However, although there are certain advantages to be gained by conducting experiments in which players are unable to communicate directly with one another, their major drawback is that there is no such prohibition ruling in the real world. Friedman,[15] for example, set up experiments involving the running of a set of complete-information duopoly games in which players were permitted to communicate by means of written messages before each decision. Once communication was permitted, the interesting question arose as to whether or not players would honour the agreements they had negotiated, and the pay-off matrix was constructed in such a way as to offer considerable rewards to players who could get away with cheating their rival.

Friedman set out to determine both the extent to which subjects could agree on a joint course of action, and also the extent to which the agreements specified Pareto-optimal points, in which circumstances no player could raise his profits without simultaneously lowering those of his rival. He found that 'Over ¾ of all the periods were periods of agreement. These were honoured in nine out of ten cases. Among the agreements better than ¾ involved Pareto optimal points.'[16]

Although the evidence forthcoming from the above experiments is by no means comprehensive or free from ambiguities[17] it appears reasonable to conclude that joint profitability can be materially improved through collusion, and, further, that the attitude of firms towards collusion will be coloured by past experience of price wars, and also by the degree of uncertainty which they face in their operations.

Furthermore, the extent of collusion can be said to depend (1) upon the number of firms within the industry, since the greater the number of firms the harder it is for any one firm to gather information about its rivals and the harder it becomes to detect secret price cutting; (2) upon the amount of information possessed by each firm about its rivals; (3) upon the height of barriers to entry; and (4) upon any differences in cost levels between firms, since the greater the difference in average cost between the most and least efficient the harder it is for the firms as a group to settle upon a mutually acceptable price.

Chapter 10

The Role of Entry in Oligopoly

(i) *Introduction*

The literature on entry has become very extensive over the years.[1] Although the question of entry-preventing behaviour was first raised by Kaldor,[2] the main discussion arose out of the basic prediction of the model of monopolistic competition that firms would earn only normal profits in the long run, and that each firm would be operating with excess capacity (see p. 37). Harrod argued[3] that firms would forgo some potential profit in the short run by setting a price lower than that which would maximise their profits in order to discourage new entrants into the industry. Subsequently, the discussion of the role of entry has largely evolved into an attempt to provide an answer to the question as to whether it is more profitable for a firm to maximise short-run profits in the knowledge that this will attract new entrants and hence erode the firm's market share in the long run, or for a firm to deter entry by holding down prices in the short run in the expectation that it will be able to retain a substantial share of the market over time. These possibilities are illustrated in Figure 10.1.

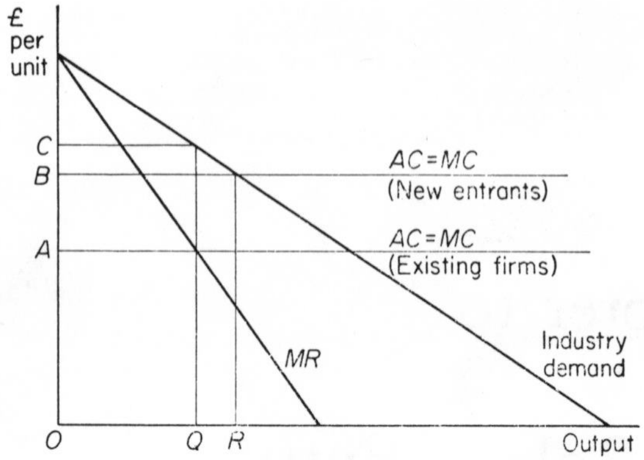

FIG. 10.1

(ii) *The Limit Price*

All established firms are assumed to operate along an identical average-cost curve (which is also the marginal-cost curve as drawn in Figure 10.1). This also applies to all new entrants, but the level of AC is higher for these firms than for those already within the industry. In Figure 10.1 where existing firms are maximising short-run profits by equating *MC* and *MR*, they sell a combined output of OQ at a price of OC. Since, however, this price exceeds the average-cost curve of potential entrants these will find it profitable to move into the industry. As a result that part of market demand satisfied by established firms will be steadily reduced, implying a shift to the left of the demand curve which they communally face, and hence a lowering of price. As more and more new firms enter the industry so price steadily falls until it reaches a level of *OB*, whereupon it ceases to be profitable for any additional firms to enter the industry. This price of *OB* is known as the *limit price* since it is the price at which entry ceases. It should be noted that whereas new entrants are making only normal profits in the long run (AR=AC), established firms are still making some super-normal profits (*OB*—OA per unit) although considerably less than they were making in the short run (OC—OA per unit). The ability of established firms to retain super-normal profits in the long run is a function of the *barriers to entry* within the industry which make it possible for established firms to operate along a lower average-cost curve than potential entrants.

Suppose, however, that established firms decide to prevent entry by holding price down below the profit-maximising level in the short run. Any price greater than OB will clearly lead to the entry of new firms because it will enable them to make a super-normal profit. The highest price that will prevent entry is therefore OB, and at that price established firms can sell a communal output of OR at a profit level of AB per unit both in the short and in the long run (because entry is prevented).

But we have already noted that profit-maximising firms earn a profit of AC per unit in the short run and AB per unit in the long run, so why should the entry-preventing strategy ever be selected? The answer is, of course, that whereas the profit per unit is indeed in the short run higher than, and in the long run identical with, that of an entry-preventing firm, the latter firm sells a larger output even in the short run, as explained above. Furthermore, the output differential between a profit-maximising and an entry-preventing firm increases steadily over time because the former's demand curve is shifting progressively to the left as more and more firms enter the industry. It also follows that the number of firms within the industry is smaller when entry is prevented than when it is free, and hence that an industry which exhibits entry-preventing behaviour tends to be quite highly concentrated.

(iii) *Conditions of Entry*

The seminal work on entry to which most importance is currently attached is that of Bain[4] and Sylos-Labini.[5] Sylos-Labini concentrated almost exclusively upon homogeneous oligopoly whereby all firms, whether actual or potential, produce perfectly substitutable commodities while operating along identical average-cost curves. As a result, the only exploitable barrier to entry stems from access to economies of scale.[6] Bain, however, also considered the possible existence of competing products (the product-differentiation-barrier to entry) and the possible existence of a variety of average-cost curves along which different firms operated (the absolute-cost-advantage barrier to entry).

Now clearly if there are no barriers to entry whatsoever this is analogous to perfect competition, and there can be no incentive to prevent entry, since any lowering of price by existing firms below the average cost of potential entrants necessarily also lowers it below their own. This can be referred to as a condition of *easy entry*. Three further possibilities exist:[7]

(1) There are limited barriers to entry which result in an established firm operating at an average cost only slightly below that of potential entrants – Bain referred to this possibility as *ineffectively impeded entry*;

(2) there are substantial barriers to entry which result in established firms operating at an average cost considerably below that of potential entrants – Bain referred to this possibility as *effectively impeded entry*; and

(3) barriers to entry are so substantial, and established firms' cost advantage so great that the higher price in the short run is that which impedes entry rather than that which maximises profits.[8] This Bain referred to as *blockaded entry*.

In this latter case firms can maximise short-run profits without losing part of their markets to new entrants. In the case of easy entry new entrants cannot be excluded so profit maximisation is the best short-run strategy. This is also the optimal strategy in ineffectively impeded entry because limit pricing in such circumstances allows established firms to make only a very small margin of super-normal profit. However, if entry is effectively impeded, limit pricing is the optimal strategy since it will permit established firms to make appreciable super-normal profits both in the short run and in the long run.[9]

(iv) *Extensions of the Limit-Price Model*

A further consideration introduced by both Bain and Sylos-Labini, henceforth to be referred to as *Sylos's postulate*,[10] is the assumption that potential entrants behave in the expectation that established firms will adopt that policy which is least favourable to entrants, this being a policy of holding their output constant.[11] If new entrants act on this assumption then they will expect the post-entry price to fall, because the creation of new capacity will cause over-all capacity to exceed what the market can absorb. Hence a potential entrant will not proceed unless he expects the post-entry price to exceed his average cost of production, and this permits established firms to hold their price above their average cost by an amount equal to the fall in price which potential entrants expect to result from the introduction of additional capacity. It also follows that established firms can prevent entry while setting a price in excess of their average cost even where potential entrants expect to operate with a similar level of cost.

On a more general level it can be seen that the extent of actual entry, if any, depends upon the view taken of the post-entry behaviour of established firms by potential entrants. Sylos's postulate is clearly only one of many alternative hypotheses in this context. What actually happens to industry price and output once entry has taken place clearly depends upon the post-entry behaviour both of established firms and of the new entrants. This line of argument has strong parallels with the theoretical oligopoly models discussed in the preceding sections, with one small difference. Whereas previously we only considered the attitude of rivals towards other firms already within the industry, we have now extended the analysis to cover the attitudes of established firms towards potential entrants as well.

Sherman and Willett[12] noted that in its original version Sylos's postulate only took account of a single potential entrant. They developed a model to consider the implications of increasing the number of potential entrants, thereby complicating the analysis since each potential entrant's profit now depended not only upon the response of established firms but also upon whether other firms entered as well. They concluded that when there were several potential entrants, rather than one, price could easily rise above the price which would forestall entry by a single potential entrant without inducing entry.

Pashigian,[13] on the other hand, argued that 'A determined entrant could lower or eliminate the monopolist's profits by entering, and even could cause the monopolist to suffer larger losses, if he maintained output, than would the entrant. The limit price theory does not satisfactorily explain why this does not occur.' He suggested that [14] 'it seems preferable to define a limit price as that price which causes the entrant to suffer a larger present value of losses than the monopolist suffers if entry did occur'. Pashigian also questioned the assumption of the limit-price theory that the monopolist is not able to select the profit-maximising price and, yet, can block entry by threatening to lower the price if entry is attempted. However he answered this question to his own satisfaction and concluded that the monopolist was, except in rare cases, unable to have the best of both worlds.[15]

Williamson [16] observed that the limit-price theory assumed that established firms chose one or other of two well-defined alternative strategies, namely maximising short-run profits or limit pricing. He also noted that if the limit price was adopted this would suggest that established firms were willing to exclude entry at any price. In the same context Stigler argued that [17] it may be more profitable to retard the rate of entry than to forestall it completely,[18] and also that [19] if industry demand is expected to grow rapidly then potential entrants may not be put off by the prospect of poor short-run returns in view of the more promising longer-term outlook. Kamien and Schwartz [20] considered a market in which the seller is aware that his pricing policy will affect the probability of entry of competing suppliers. They concluded that 'Limit pricing, to preclude entry, appears to be optimal only in very special cases. The seller will optimally set its price somewhere below the monopoly profit-maximising price (unless the latter price precludes entry) but never so low that it would not forgo profits if entry should occur.'

Wenders [21] redefined the limit price as 'the highest pre-entry price which, after taking account of *both* the effects of the entrant and the monopolist's reaction to this entrant, will make it unprofitable for any entrant'. He argued that 'if entrants appear which either cannot be driven out or it would be comparatively unprofitable to do so, the most profitable thing for a monopolist to do is contract output in the face of actual entry'. Thus it would often be most profitable for a monopolist to permit new entrants, even if they could be excluded, where such entrants are 'few and far between and show a willingness to be co-operative'. He therefore concluded that 'If there is any kind of collusion going in the industry, the most profitable reaction for the established firms is to contract or expand output depending on the situation. It is never profitable for them to follow Sylos's postulate and do nothing.'

(v) *The Implications for Pricing Policy*

In a subsequent section (see pp. 91–8) we will be examining the full-cost pricing technique whereby prices are determined by adding to average variable cost an allowance for overheads and selling expenses, to which is added an appropriate profit margin. Now one implication of the above discussion of limit pricing is that it may well pay a firm to introduce the cost-plus in preference to the marginalist technique, using a mark-up which is as large as possible while still preventing entry. This is because if one firm's variable costs alter it is very probable that the same effects will be felt both by other established firms and by potential entrants. Hence for moderate variations in variable costs a good approximation of the new limit price can be obtained by adding to the new average variable cost the same mark-up as before. This suggests that the use of the unsophisticated cost-plus technique is suitable for all except drastic changes in variable costs which affect an entire industry, and that firms can thereby save themselves the trouble of estimating demand elasticity and marginal cost and revenue.

(vi) *Criticisms of the Model*

In our discussion of extensions of the model of limit pricing we effectively introduced a number of criticisms of the model itself in its basic formulation. We have also noted that firms within an industry find it most profitable to set a limit price only when entry is effectively impeded, and when entry lags are not great. As Osborne has pointed out,[22] however, certain conditions must be met before entry can be said to be effectively impeded. First, technology must not be rapidly changing otherwise new entrants may be able to operate newer, and hence cheaper, plant than established firms. Secondly, demand must not be growing rapidly otherwise there is room for new entrants without cutting into the sales of established firms. Thirdly, the minimum profitable output of new entrants must constitute a significant portion of industry output otherwise new entrants can move into the industry without price being much affected by the change in capacity. Finally, new entrants must suffer cost disadvantages due to, for example, product differentiation or the magnitude of capital requirements. In Osborne's opinion the theory of limit pricing 'applies to only a restricted category of markets. That is a mark against its theoretical stature, for it *at least* lacks generality'.[23]

A further difficulty surrounds the question as to whether potential entrants are affected by the pre-entry or anticipated post-entry behaviour of established firms. The limit-pricing model is based upon the presumption that potential entrants are influenced by pre-entry levels of profit, and that they are put off by the fact that established firms are not earning very much profit per unit when the limit price is in operation. Furthermore, if Sylos's postulate applies, potential entrants do not expect to earn any super-normal profits at all once entry has taken place. But if Sylos's postulate does not apply, and potential entrants have less reason to expect established firms to react adversely to their entry, the validity of the limit-pricing model becomes suspect.

It is also important to remember that limit pricing assumes that established firms will act collusively in order to prevent entry. Where products are standardised this seems a not unreasonable assumption, but its validity must be in question where products are differentiated. It is true that product differentiation appears as a barrier to entry in the limit-pricing model but, in so far as the extent of differentiation varies from firm to firm, some may feel much less threatened than others by potential entrants, and hence may feel less urgency in responding to the pressure for the setting of a limit price.

Finally, it is important to remember that there can be a wide range of possible reasons for the failure of established firms to maximise their short-run profits other than that they are limit pricing. For this reason, as we shall discover in the following section, attempts to provide empirical evidence for the existence of limit pricing concentrate upon the relationship between barriers to entry and profits, since a close relationship between these variables is more likely to lend support to the limit-pricing hypothesis than to other explanations of non-profit-maximising behaviour. Nevertheless, we must take care not to discount other factors which produce non-profit-maximising behaviour when assessing the validity of the limit-pricing model.

(vii) *The Empirical Evidence on Entry*

The seminal work on barriers to entry was conducted by Bain.[24] He classified such barriers as 'very high', 'substantial', and 'moderate-to-low' (the lowest four-firm concentration ratio being 27 per cent), and assessed their influence upon profit rates in a sample of oligopolistic industries for the periods 1936–40 and 1947–57. Bain expected to find a close similarity between the profit-maximising price and the limit price in the very high barrier class, and for the limit price to fall progressively below the profit-maximising price in line with decreases in the height-of-entry barriers. His expectation, therefore, was that profit rates would be closely correlated with the height-of-entry barriers. His findings showed a significant difference between the average profit rates of industries in the very high barrier class and those in the other categories, but not between industries in the substantial and moderate-to-low categories. He concluded [25] that 'seller concentration alone is not an adequate indicator of the probable incidence of extremes of excess profits and monopolistic output restriction. The concurrent influence of the condition of entry should clearly be taken into account.'

Mann [26] followed up Bain's study by examining the relationship between seller concentration, barriers to entry, and profit rates for the period 1950–60. He examined thirty industries of which seventeen had appeared in Bain's work, and employed an identical classification of entry barriers to that set out above. In general his results supported those of Bain. He found that there was 'a distinct cleavage between the average profit rates of the two groups of industries, divided according to whether the concentration ratio for the eight firms is greater or less than 70 per cent'.[27] He also found [28] 'a distinct difference between the average profit rates of the very high barrier group and the other two classes. A difference occurred between the substantial and moderate-to-low barrier classes, but it was less than one half of the difference between the very high and the substantial barrier categories.' In view of the failure to distinguish clearly between these latter two categories he concluded that 'The limit price hypothesis, then, remains neither confirmed nor rejected'.[29] His final finding was that 'barriers to entry apparently exert an independent influence in that highly concentrated industries with very high barriers to entry earned a distinctly higher average return than highly concentrated industries in other categories'.

Mann's article sparked off a lengthy interchange [30] about the validity of his findings, without proving particularly conclusive either way. McGuckin [31] subsequently found that 'high concentration by itself appears to offer no guarantees against entry and a subsequent loss of market shares by large firms', and in an examination of the U.S. automobile industry Wenders [32] found that pricing policy was consistent with limit pricing but not with short-run profit maximisation. In the latest study to be conducted Orr [33] concluded, on the basis of Canadian evidence, that 'Barriers to entry permit higher profits, and a given increase in profit rates attracts fewer entrants in a high-barrier than a low-barrier industry. A difference between observed and entry limiting profit rates will attract fewer entrants in a high-barrier than a low-barrier industry'.

In general we must go along with Low's conclusion [34] that 'studies to date have shown very little concerning the prevalence of limit pricing in the economy. And the remaining empirical evidence – showing firms whose profit, pricing and output policies do not conform to traditional profit maximisation assumptions – is open to alternate explanations'.

Part 2

Alternative Theories of the Firm

Chapter 11

Introduction

As we have seen in the preceding sections that most of the models which together comprise the theory of oligopoly draw heavily upon the concepts and relationships between variables which constitute the basic building blocks of the traditional models of the firm. Of particular importance in this respect was the continued adherence of oligopoly models to the objective of profit maximisation despite the accumulation of contradictory evidence.

Now the accepted rule for identifying a firm's profit-maximising output is that it should equate marginal cost with marginal revenue. But can a firm be expected to identify its cost and revenue curves with any great precision except under conditions of perfect knowledge about its own operations and those of its competitors? We must presume not, yet if the real world is characterised more by widespread uncertainty than by perfect knowledge, considerable doubt must be thrown upon the ability of a firm to achieve its chosen objective.

But even if we do permit the assumption of perfect knowledge to stand, what evidence is there that the typical firm's cost and revenue schedules bear any resemblance in real life to those postulated in the traditional models of the firm? And is it realistic to go along with the traditional assumption that price is highly responsive to changing conditions of demand in the market-place? We have suggested a partial answer to this latter question during our review of the theory of oligopoly. Nevertheless, we have reached the point in our analysis of the theory of the firm when we must call into question even the most hallowed precepts of the traditional theory of the firm.

In the sections which follow immediately upon this introduction we will use the results of empirical studies to try and answer the questions raised above: first, we will consider the assumptions of perfect knowledge contained in the traditional theory of the firm; secondly, the assumption of U-shaped cost curves; and thirdly, the assumption that price is determined by demand rather than cost conditions.

By the time that we have finished such investigations it will have become abundantly clear that any theory which hopes to be able to predict the behaviour of modern industrial firms must follow a different line of reasoning to that of traditional theory. The most important factor in this respect, however, is unquestionably the choice of the firm's objective function, since if we retain the objective of profit maximisation then it is still possible to put forward the argument that even if a firm operates in an uncertain environment, and even if it uses rules of thumb in preference to marginal analysis, provided all firms are in the same boat they will still be able to reach an end state closely approximating to that of profit maximisation.

To most post-war commentators, however, it appears at best illogical to argue that, although a firm's operating circumstances diverge substantially from those postulated in traditional models of the firm, the same conclusion will be reached. Rather, they prefer to believe that the typical modern corporation pursues objectives other than profit maximisation, and that this is the cause of, for example, the divergence of currently observable pricing policy from that postulated in traditional theory. Unfortunately, however, that is often as far as agreement goes between the various schools of thought, and there are now almost as many alternative objective functions postulated for the firm as there are commentators on business affairs.

The latter part of this book is given over to an examination of some of the most influential of the models which postulate objectives other than the maximisation of profits. These we will refer to generically as 'alternative theories of the firm'. Our discussion of these theories would not, however, be complete, without prior examination of the hypothesis of the separation of ownership from control, which is trotted out in almost every case in order to justify the downgrading of the profit objective among large firms. The nub of the argument is simply that, whereas shareholder control is synonymous with profit-maximising behaviour, management control is synonymous with other, less-profitable, objectives. Far too often this hypothesis is treated as too obvious to warrant further comment. This issue is, however, treated fully in this text.

Chapter 12

Economies of Scale and Average Cost

(i) *Introduction*

The shape of the average-cost curve is determined by the relationship between total cost and the scale of output. The U-shaped average-cost curve which appeared in the traditional models of perfect competition and monopoly reflected the assumption that a firm would initially have access to economies of scale, but that after a time any further expansion of output would cause average cost to rise as diseconomies of scale set in.

That the average-cost curve should be U-shaped was especially important in the case of the perfectly competitive model. In that model the firm's long-run optimal output was defined as the point at which the horizontal average-revenue (demand) curve was tangential to the average-cost curve at the latter's lowest point, and only one point of tangency was therefore possible. However, were the average-cost curve to become horizontal beyond a certain level of output then there would no longer be a single point of tangency. This is because the average-revenue and average-cost curves would not merely be tangential but identical along the flat section of the average-cost curve, to which a firm should necessarily respond by continually increasing output. But such a firm would eventually grow sufficiently large so as to affect market price, in which event a necessary precondition for the existence of perfect competition would be abrogated.

(ii) *Empirical Cost Studies*

Many attempts have been made to provide empirical evidence relating to the relationship between changes in scale and average cost, with the intention in most cases of supporting the hypothesis that average cost either falls, or is constant, over a firm's normal output range. We generally refer in this context to the L-shaped average-cost curve. The bulk of the evidence to which we refer below relates to long-run average cost, although certain studies have concentrated upon short-run effects.[1] These latter studies suggest that short-run average cost reaches a minimum when plant is working more or less at the full capacity for which it was designed. Subsequently squeezing additional capacity out of the plant can only be done at the expense of rapidly escalating costs.

An early study by Wiles [2] which summarised a good deal of evidence about the shape of the long-run average-cost curve (*LRAC*) typified the conclusions drawn by supporters of the L-shaped *LRAC*. He concluded that

> the long-run average-cost curve descends like the left-hand branch of a capital U, swiftly at first and then more gently. Decreasing costs with size are almost universal. But the U seldom turns up again. Sharply increasing costs with size are practically unknown, and even slight increases are rare. Sixty per cent of the examples obey what we may call the law of L-shaped costs. Another 31 per cent show a slight increase of costs in the largest size class. Most but by no means all of these slight increases are well within the expected margin of error that any empirical correlation should show.

There are, however, considerable computational difficulties in determining the shape of the *LRAC*. We must therefore stop to consider at this point the three [3] main methods of estimating the *LRAC* and their respective drawbacks. These methods are known respectively as (i) statistical cost analysis, (ii) engineering estimates, and the (iii) survivor technique.

(iii) *Statistical Cost Analysis*

This technique is based upon data concerning the actual production costs of making a particular good in plant of various sizes. A major study based upon evidence derived through the employment of this technique was conducted by Johnston.[4] He concluded that the most notable common element of this evidence was 'the preponderance of the L-shaped pattern of long-run average cost that emerges so frequently from the various long-run analyses'.

Quite clearly this technique can only be employed if there are a relatively large number of firms producing the product under examination since each separate plant yields only one point on the *LRAC*. But even if this condition is satisfied the technique is subject to many drawbacks. First, it assumes that each output studied is the optimal output for that plant or firm, and this condition is not frequently met with in practice. Secondly, it assumes that the various plants and firms are all utilising the same technology. But if firms enter the industry at different times and always employ the latest technology while existing firms stick to the old, then statistical cost analysis will not yield a *LRAC* which reflects the most efficient known methods. It is also necessary that firms depreciate their fixed assets at a uniform rate and that they employ uniform accounting methods if costs are to be strictly comparable. Finally, it is possible that if, for example, a firm continues to work outdated and inefficient equipment until it wears out before replacing it with new and efficient equipment, statistical cost analysis will yield data on the short-run rather than long-run average cost for that firm while simultaneously yielding non-comparable data on *LRAC* for other firms within the industry.[5]

(iv) *Engineering Estimates*

The engineering technique involves the estimation of what the costs of producing various levels of output would be, irrespective of whether or not any firm is actually producing at these output levels. Past and present cost data serve as a basis for these estimates, although there is necessarily an element of subjectivity involved in estimating the *LRAC* of output levels not currently being produced by existing firms.[6]

The results of engineering studies indicate that the *LRAC* of a product tends initially to fall and subsequently to level out. The point at which *LRAC* becomes horizontal is the product's minimum efficient scale of operation. In a few instances, such as the aircraft industry, the market is insufficiently large for even one firm of efficient size to operate within it, so that *LRAC* is falling over each firm's normal output range. In those cases where *LRAC* does level out we can determine the largest number of efficient firms which a market can absorb by dividing total market size by the minimum efficient output. If this number turns out to be small then high efficiency can only be attained at the cost of a substantial degree of monopoly power.

It is difficult to draw hard and fast conclusions on the extent of economies of scale in U.K. industry on the basis of engineering estimates. As with other methods of calculating *LRAC*, engineering estimates are subject to a number of drawbacks, amongst the most important of which is the inherent difficulty of obtaining cost information in a form suitable for analysis. Perhaps the fairest conclusion is that reached by Silberston [7] who defines 'significant' scale effects to apply to markets where the cost disadvantages of operating below minimum efficient scale are considerable (that is the *LRAC* slopes down steeply before reaching the point at which it levels out), and where capital and other entry costs are high. In his opinion [8] 'it is probably fair to conclude that there are comparatively few industries which have significant economies of scale in this sense, in relation always to the size of the market'.

(v) *Survivor Technique*

The survivor technique broadly suggests that, over the course of time, only the most efficient firms will survive within an industry. The way in which the survivor technique might be applied is (1) to list all firms within an industry according to their output, (2) to select appropriate output ranges, and (3) to then add up the percentage share of the industry's output produced by each output range. Logic then suggests that any output range which, over time, increases its share of total output, is doing so at the expense of firms within other output ranges. Hence the conclusion is drawn that firms falling within the expanding output range must be the most efficient, and that they are operating along the lowest part of the long-run average-cost curve.

Obviously this optimal output range may vary over time, so that this technique can only be applied if data are available over relatively long periods of time. Also, there needs to be a sufficiently large number of firms within the industry for the results to be statistically significant.

Attempts to apply the survivor technique have been made by Stigler,[9] Saving,[10] Weiss[11] and Shepherd,[12] the technique being applicable to firms as well as to plants. Stigler, for example, investigated the U.S. steel industry, particularly those firms using open-hearth or Bessemer processes. He concluded that the range of optimum plant size was between ¾ per cent and 10 per cent of the industry's capacity, while the range of optimum firm size was between 2½ per cent and 25 per cent of the industry's capacity.

The above studies are all in fairly general agreement about the relationship between scale and efficiency in most industries. Saving[13] expresses it thus:

> An analysis of the survivorship estimates of optimum size of plant yielded the following conclusions: (a) both the mean optimum size and the minimum optimum size are usually small when compared with their respective industry sizes; (b) the range of optimum size is usually large relative to its respective mean optimum size (c) in those industries in which the plants compete in national markets optimum size is rarely so large as to necessitate non-competitive industry behaviour (d) the primary determinants of optimum size are the industry size and capital intensiveness.

The survivor technique has in its turn been subjected to extensive criticism.[14] It has been argued, for example, that there is little direct correlation between efficiency and survival. It has also been suggested[15] that 'Firms experiencing reductions in the share of industry output may be just as efficient but may face slightly different economic environments which prevent them from growing as rapidly as other firms; alternatively, the objectives of such firms may involve lower growth rates than other firms having the same unit costs'.

Chapter 13

Pricing Behaviour[1]

(i) *Introduction*

Traditional models of the firm all incorporate the objective of profit maximisation. Furthermore, these models stipulate that the price–output combination which satisfies this objective is identified by recourse to the rule that marginal cost should be equated with marginal revenue. Hence the traditional models of the firm can be seen to require accurate data on both cost *and* demand conditions for the purposes of price determination.

However, empirical research into pricing methods,[2] largely a post-war phenomenon, has tended to produce results at variance with the traditional hypothesis outlined above.

(ii) *Cost-Plus Pricing*

The literature on pricing behaviour has for the most part concentrated upon pricing methods based upon costs, at present most commonly referred to as *cost-plus* pricing. This expression has several synonyms. In its earliest guise it was known as *administered* pricing, and the controversy generated by Dr Means's seminal paper [3] has by no means yet died down.[4] Currently it is also known as *full-cost*, *mark-up*, and *target-rate-of-return* pricing. The difference between, for example, mark-up and full-cost pricing can be outlined as follows. In mark-up pricing the mark-up is generally added to variable costs without any attempt being made to allocate overhead expenses to individual items, often simply because of the difficulties involved in conducting such an allocation with any degree of accuracy. In full-cost pricing, on the other hand, variable costs are added to an allowance for overheads, and for marketing expenses where appropriate, and the mark-up is applied to the sum total of these costs.

Mark-ups can be either fixed or flexible. Where they are fixed then prices only remain unchanged provided unit costs also remain unchanged, since if costs vary, a fixed mark-up must result in changing prices. Where, however, a firm requires prices to remain unchanged irrespective of cost conditions, because, for example, its competitors follow such a procedure, it will have to employ flexible mark-ups which vary inversely with costs.

Closely allied to full-cost pricing is pricing in order to achieve a target rate of return on investment, which was found by the Brookings study [5] to be the commonest pricing policy employed by very large firms in the United States. The technique used to achieve a long-run target return is to calculate the appropriate mark-up on full costs according to the formula,

$$\text{percentage mark-up} = \text{target return on investment} \times \frac{\text{average capital employed}}{\text{cost of sales}}$$

The cost of sales is calculated on the basis of a 'standard' or 'normal' level of output, which is expressed as a percentage of available capacity. The calculation, is, however, subject to one severe drawback which derives from the failure to take demand conditions into consideration. In target pricing, the firm calculates its 'standard' output and the costs associated with it, and applies whatever is the appropriate mark-up needed in order to achieve its chosen target return. The price–output combination thrown up by this procedure may not, however, be anywhere along the demand curve for the product. The price set by the firm is itself a determinant of demand, and there is no automatic mechanism to ensure that, at the selected price, the firm will be able to dispose of its standard output, no more and no less. Failure to sell its standard output implies that unit cost per good sold will, in practice, be different from that which was inserted into the above formula, and hence that the actual return on sales will differ from the target return.

The pricing techniques outlined above are also subject to other drawbacks. There is, for example, no uniformity across firms as to the cost conventions used as the basis for price setting. Some firms may use standard costs and others either historic or expected costs (that is past or present cost levels extrapolated into the future). No cost convention typically utilised by a firm's accountants may, however, be appropriate. It may, for example, be more profitable for a firm to operate in the short run at a price sufficient only to cover variable costs, in the hope of utilising spare capacity or deterring prospective competitors.[6]

It is also argued that pricing policies which largely ignore the elasticity of demand are unlikely to lead to profit maximisation (assuming of course, that such is the firm's objective). In many markets demand may vary considerably on either a seasonal or cyclical basis, and the strength of demand also tends to vary considerably over the product's life span. This criticism applies more readily to fixed mark-ups, which are wholly insensitive to demand conditions, than to flexible mark-ups which can be adjusted periodically to suit changing market conditions. Indeed, it is argued that it will not generally pay a firm to try to maximise short-run profits by too frequently altering price in order to charge what the market will bear. First of all this may alienate customers and cause loss of goodwill, and hence reduce profits in the longer term. Also, where a firm sells a wide range of products, it is both time-consuming and expensive to be constantly adjusting price lists.

Another advantage claimed for cost-plus pricing methods is that they obviate the necessity to estimate demand elasticities under conditions of uncertainty (see also pp. 99–100), a process the costs of which may outweigh the benefits. It is also suggested that many firms are satisficers rather than profit maximisers (see pp. 135–6), and that cost-plus pricing enables a firm to earn a fair level of profits while providing customers with good value for money. However, those firms which utilise flexible mark-ups do appear to be trying to avoid giving their customers too good a deal, and it can be argued that most of the variability in mark-ups is a response to changing demand conditions, such that cost-plus pricing can be expected to lead to long-run profit maximisation.[7]

(iii) *Empirical Pricing Studies*

The best-known seminal work is that of Hall and Hitch[8] who interviewed 38 entrepreneurs running firms which could be described as oligopolistic. They concluded that most of the entrepreneurs were unfamiliar with marginal analysis and that they were anyway not seeking to maximise profits in the short run. They mostly relied upon some variant of cost-plus pricing although they were generally of the opinion that, in the long run, this would take them reasonably near to maximising their profits, given the need to make allowances for competitive reactions. They felt that it was fairer to all concerned not to try to maximise short-run profits. Now and again certain entrepreneurs raised or lowered their prices when demand conditions were significantly altered, but for the most part prices were held constant, implying flexible mark-ups on costs (and hence a substantial degree of open or tacit collusion). The authors concluded[9] that 'most of our informants were vague about anything so precise as elasticity . . . in addition many, perhaps most, apparently made no effort, even implicitly, to estimate elasticities of demand . . . and of those who do the majority considered the information of little or no relevance to the pricing process save perhaps in very exceptional conditions.'

Professor Pearce,[10] while acknowledging that prices were based upon costs and that profit margins tended to remain stable, argued that 'What is less generally known, except to those who practice the art of price fixing, is how often and for what a variety of reasons "normal" profit is not in fact charged against any particular sale . . . Margins charged are highly sensitive to the market under normally competitive conditions, and the "norm" is simply that figure around which they fluctuate.'

Pearce investigated one medium-sized U.K. manufacturing firm using questionnaires and interviews, and recorded both quoted prices and actual selling prices. He concluded that a wide variation existed between the profit margins as discussed in interviews and the way in which they turned out in practice, and that individual products did not produce consistent profit levels.

Earley set out[11] to infer from indirect evidence whether or not two non-marginalist hypotheses were true: first, one which claimed that a firm has 'predominantly a long-run and defensive viewpoint in its pricing, production and investment policies (rather than an alert attitude towards its near at hand profit opportunities)', and secondly, that it uses 'in the main a full-cost rather than incremental cost calculus in its pricing, production and investment decisions'. He concluded, as a result of an extensive survey of 217 manufacturing companies rated as 'excellently managed' by the American Institute of Management that 'judged either by responses to individual questions or the foregoing component indexes, the evidence of overall marginalism among companies is very strong . . . Approximately 60 per cent of them show what can be considered from "substantial" to very strong marginalism'. He also considered that 'short views, innovative sensitivity, marginal costing and marginal pricing are all preponderant among the responding companies'; that 'where considerable segmented variable cost data are brought to management's attention the companies short-range policies are consistent with their longer-range costing, pricing, and other product related policies'; and finally that 'with such companies marginalism is apparently not dependent upon, though it is increased by, a short time perspective'.

Hague,[12] however, points out that the results of this kind of study 'depend too much on inferences and implications read into personal opinions expressed verbally by businessmen and too little on authentic written statements and statistical data'. On the other hand, this objection largely applies to his own study in which he interviewed eight large and twelve small firms in the Black Country. He found that the firms were less interested in profit maximisation than in 'a comfortable and secure income'. Two distinct types of output policy were found. 'In small firms output was rarely fixed so as to equate marginal cost and marginal revenue, but by rule-of-thumb methods. In large firms on the other hand there was a greater desire to earn maximum profits . . . but again there was no attempt at careful balancing of marginal revenue and marginal cost. In general these firms seemed to be satisfied that long-run profits were maximised, but they had no scientific policy for ensuring this.'

Hague also found that where there was no conventional or controlled price for the article, firms based price upon what appeared in general to be the accountant's estimate of 'total unit cost' (which is much the same thing as Hall and Hitch's notion of 'full-cost') to which was added a profit margin based largely on convention.

The findings of the Brookings study, originally conducted between 1948 and 1957, but subsequently updated, were primarily based upon the pricing practices as reported by representative firms in all sectors of big business, including primary production, distribution and manufacturing. The basic technique used was the interview, which, as was pointed out in the study, is not the most reliable way of obtaining information. However, this is unlikely to have seriously affected the validity of the results, which in general indicated that the firms in question invariably sought to earn satisfactory profits, and that they often felt themselves to be approximating to profit-maximising behaviour in the long run. The firms did not consider that profit maximisation as a goal had any operational implications for pricing policy, although it was not necessarily incorrect to suppose that they would not achieve it in the end. The authors observed [13] that, 'for the most part the companies doubted that by changing their pricing policies they could raise their profits in the long run'.

The authors found it appropriate to cluster the respondents' avowed pricing policies into five groups, into one of which each firm could be slotted although most firms did not keep rigidly to only one approach to pricing irrespective of market circumstances. The first of these groups was referred to as *pricing to achieve a target return on investment*. This approach was adopted by over one-third of the companies interviewed, which for the most part adopted the basic cost-plus formula previously described although 'the discussions of policy also disclosed that among those that could be characterised in general as following an administered, stabilised, cost-plus system of pricing, the degree of precision and of compliance ranged too widely to make target return a master key to pricing'.[14]

Target-return pricing was particularly popular with firms which either operated in industries characterised by entry barriers or which were introducing new products, since in neither case was much competition to be expected. This is borne out by other studies. The evidence has been assessed by Baldwin as follows.[15] 'Very crudely we should expect to find a positive correlation between the height of barriers to entry and use of target rate of return pricing unless entry is blockaded', where *blockaded* entry results where the price which would attract new entrants is above the profit-maximising price of the most favoured firm currently in the industry.

Lanzillotti, in his follow-up to the Brookings study [16] noted a wide range of explanations for the choice of a specific target return as follows:

(1) The most frequently mentioned rationalisations included (*a*) fair or reasonable return, (*b*) the traditional industry concept of fair return in relation to risk factors, (*c*) desire to equal or better the corporation average return over a recent period, (*d*) what the company felt it could get as a long-run matter, and (*e*) use of a specific profit target as a means of stabilising industry prices;

(2) The next most popular approach to pricing was *stabilisation of price and margin*, which was defined by the U.S. Steel Corporation as 'selling at the lowest price consistent with cost and a reasonable profit'. The other approaches were *pricing to reflect product differentiation, pricing to meet or match competition*, and *pricing to maintain or improve market share* respectively.[17]

Several years after the publication of the Bookings study of pricing in large firms, Haynes[18] conducted a parallel investigation for small firms employing, for the most part, fewer than 200 employees. 88 firms were investigated, predominantly from the manufacturing, retailing and service sectors of the U.S. economy. His conclusions were broadly as follows:

(1) prices were more often based upon costs rather than upon demand;

(2) 'mark-up' pricing was common, particularly in retailing firms;

(3) mark-ups were set at different levels for different groups of products;

(4) price leadership by large firms made many small firms price followers; and

(5) information on costs and demand was often poor, making it difficult for the firms to apply pricing rules.

In a study of 139 Danish firms Fog[19] also found that some variant of full-cost pricing was especially common. In another study, Cyert and March[20] tested the cost-plus rule by predicting the price which, on the basis of cost information, they expected a department store to charge for 197 randomly selected goods. They found that in 188 cases they had predicted the selling price to the nearest cent.

Skinner[21] sent out a postal questionnaire to all members of the Merseyside Chamber of Commerce in early 1968. His main conclusion[22] was that 'although 70 per cent of the respondents in the survey claim to use cost-plus pricing, great weight is given in fixing prices to competition and demand, although not quite as much weight as to a firm's own cost and profits.

In his study Skinner asked firms whether they divided their costs into fixed and variable elements, and, if so, whether the distinction provided the basis for price setting. 73 per cent claimed to make the distinction, and 69 per cent to use it for price setting. Skinner then went on to argue (on similar lines to Earley), that a firm which makes this distinction is employing variable (otherwise known as 'marginal') costing. Sizer,[23] however, thinks that 'A more reasonable interpretation of Skinner's results may be that firms analyse costs into fixed and variable elements as part of the procedure for establishing overhead recovery rates and mark up on cost percentages'.

Clearly there are certain semantic difficulties involved in the task of treating published studies on a compatible basis. Silberston has attempted to do this, and concludes that [24]

full cost can be given a mark of beta query plus, but no more than this since there are so many marginalist and behavioural qualifications. It seems clear that the procedure of calculating prices very often starts with an average cost type of calculation, but the qualifications that arise are concerned with the next stage of the process, including the exact method by which full costs are calculated. An important point to remember is that the studies mentioned concentrate mainly on home market prices, and that there is abundant evidence that in export pricing, marginal calculations figure much more prominently.

Chapter 14

Imperfections of Information

The crux of the problem has been expressed by Margolis as follows:[1]

The information and calculability necessary for the management of a firm to move to its equilibrium profit-maximising price–output combination are clearly not available. Uncertainty and ignorance are omni-present. No matter how pleasing may be the prospect of an activity with the greatest possible profits, the choice for management is rarely on the agenda.

Uncertainty arises simply because the outcome of a decision will only become known some time into the future, and the future can rarely be predicted with perfect foresight. Hence a policy which is chosen by a firm because it appears to offer the prospect of maximum profits may turn out, in practice, to earn very little profit or even no profit at all.

However, even where the outcome of various alternative projects can be predicted with certainty, the project which seemingly offers the prospect of greatest profits may turn out to be a costly mistake because of imperfections in the data on which the profit estimates were made.

The acquisition of detailed information is, anyway, a costly business for a firm. Furthermore, the process of information retrieval often turns out to be more expensive than is necessary because the wrong information is obtained and is subsequently stored away never to be used again. Thus a firm needs to trade off the increased costs of obtaining information against the anticipated additional benefits which it expects one project to yield over and above the benefits obtainable from the next-best project. In many cases, given the uncertainty surrounding the outcome of most projects, the trade-off will come down in favour of not searching out information.

There are further difficulties where the information appears in an unsuitable form for comparisons to be made between projects. The economist's view of relevant costs differs from that of the accountant [2] whereas cost data will invariably be supplied by the latter. Reliance upon accounting data may produce a distorted picture of the costs and benefits of individual projects. But, even where the data comes in the most suitable form for project selection, the manager must himself prove capable both of recognising this to be true and also of placing the correct interpretation upon the data.

Finally, we may note that information always relates to previous time periods rather than to the present. It takes time to collect information, to process it, and to set in motion decisions based upon it. Such delays may at times result in a decision being taken in circumstances which no longer correspond to reality. The extent to which this criticism applies obviously depends upon the variability of the firm's environment.

Uncertainty and lack of knowledge can thus help account for such practices as full-cost pricing, since this technique requires relatively unsophisticated and readily available information.

Gordon [3] aptly summarised many of the above difficulties when he wrote

> Most of my criticisms centre around the fact that the tool box of formal marginalism is not very useful in a business world characterized by as much ignorance and uncertainty as do in fact prevail. These characteristics in turn stem primarily from two conditions; unending and unpredictable change and the existence of more 'directions of adjustment' (variables to be manipulated) than the businessman can possibly handle in the manner assumed in formal theory. If adjustments could be made once and for all, or if conditions would change only at long intervals, the businessman might be able to adjust marginally among alternatives theoretically available. But uninterrupted change makes physically impossible the continuous manipulation of

all the relevant variables, even if the results of all alternative lines of action could be known with certainty. Uncertainty compounds this ignorance and adds the complication of future contingencies, independent of present action that must be prepared for.

(i) *The New Microeconomics of Information and Uncertainty*

The past few years have witnessed an upsurge of renewed interest in traditional models of the firm. We have already noted that these models share the assumption of perfect knowledge, and that this assumption has been extensively criticised. The modern reformulations of these models retain the bulk of their underlying assumptions but explicitly allow for the existence of uncertainty.

The bulk of the literature concentrates upon atomistically competitive markets.[4] These are essentially markets in which strong competition prevails, but in which the diffusion of information is not instantaneous. As a result, individual firms can find themselves with transient monopoly power. This means that a firm will not immediately lose all of its customers as the result of a price rise, nor will it immediately obtain the entire market if it lowers its price. Given time, however, there will be a diffusion of new knowledge throughout the market, and a new equilibrium price will be established which is the same for all sellers.

The question then arises as to whether firms will take advantage of their transient power. On the one hand, it may be felt that exploiting the market by raising prices will increase short-run profits, but only at the expense of a loss of profits in the long run because the ensuing loss of customer goodwill will drive customers into the arms of other suppliers once all prices are again equalised. On the other hand, the short-run benefit may be felt to outweigh the long-run cost. Alternatively, a firm may, or may not, consider it worthwhile to reduce prices in the short run on the grounds that, given the eventual re-establishment of an equilibrium price, its best interests lie in attracting additional customers who will stay with the firm even in the long run because lower prices will not be obtainable elsewhere.

Phelps and Winter,[5] for example, have developed a model in which 'the individual firm believes that maintaining a constant discrepancy between its price and the prevailing industry price will result in a constant geometric growth or decline in its share of the customers'. This leads to a prediction that [6]

The firm sets its price both with an eye to the price it believes other firms are charging and to the number of customers it is serving; when it has less business than it wants, it shades its price relative to the rest of the industry. It is content to charge the prevailing price when its output level represents an appropriate balancing of the gains from more business and the costs of acquiring it through temporary price concessions.

However, it is not possible at the present time to draw any generalised conclusions about the fruitfulness of this approach. This stems from the fact that individual studies have tended so far to proceed in isolation of each other. Recognition of the interrelatedness of these studies, brought together under the generic title of the 'new microeconomics', suggests that this situation may soon be remedied.

Chapter 15

The Separation of Ownership from Control

(i) *Introduction*

There exist a number of theories which set out to explain the devices used to control corporations. Some amongst them, such as the theory of 'People's Capitalism' which claims that ownership, and hence control, is vested in the large numbers of ordinary people who own shares, and the theory of the 'Corporate Rich' which claims that control is vested in a coalition of the old propertied rich and the new managerial classes,[1] have never really caught on. Two other theories, however, are worthy of note; the first claims that control is vested in financial intermediaries of all kinds such as banks and unit trusts,[2] while the second claims that control is vested in the management of the corporation itself.

This latter theory is frequently referred to as the theory of the separation of ownership from control. It broadly states that, for various reasons, prominent among them the inability of any one individual to raise sufficient funds by himself to ensure his company's long-term growth, most large private companies are eventually forced to issue shares to the general public. Furthermore, it becomes increasingly difficult for one individual to exercise all of the managerial functions of a growing firm, so that he has increasingly to look to professional managers for assistance. Over a long period of years the number both of shareholders and of managers tends to grow, and although in principle the managers remain wholly responsible to the shareholders who own the company, they must be left to their own devices so far as the day-to-day running of the company is concerned.

In principle we would expect the objectives of management to coincide with those of the shareholders who are effectively their employers. In practice, however, the separation of ownership from control permits the managers to pursue goals other than that of profit maximisation. But the achievement of these other goals is incompatible with the simultaneous achievement of the goal of profit maximisation, with the result that the wishes of the shareholders become subservient to those of the management. Shareholders may either remain unaware that this is happening, or may be unable to do anything about it. This arises from the fact that there are, typically, a very large number of small shareholders in a modern corporation, few of whom take any sort of active interest in the way in which the company is being run. It is common knowledge that very few shareholders bother to attend their company's Annual General Meeting (A.G.M.) unless controversial matters are on the agenda, although the A.G.M. is traditionally the time for the presentation of the previous year's accounts and for the re-election of the Board of Directors. Thus, provided only that the declared dividend is not unforgivably low, the management is always able, with the assistance of a few friendly shareholders, to get the accounts accepted and to ensure the election of the desired candidates to the Board of Directors.

Furthermore, even where the shareholders are disturbed by the poor performance of the company, and as a result turn up in force to question the management at the A.G.M., their powers are strictly limited. Much though the shareholders might wish to dismiss the managers responsible for the company's performance they will realise that to do so would severely disrupt the continuity of the company's operations and thus create more problems than it solves. Thus, in essence, owners and managers are two distinct groups, each having different objectives, with those of the management predominating subject only to the proviso that shareholders' interests are not too often abused.

It is widely acknowledged that the theory of the separation of ownership from control has its roots in a classic publication by Berle and Means [3] who suggested that 'ownership is so widely distributed that no one individual or small group has even a minority interest large enough to dominate the affairs of the company'. Their study was, however, less than rigorous and took a legalistic rather than an economic interpretation of the meaning of control, since they basically set out to demonstrate that shareholders have no legally enforceable rights over their managers. Since Berle and Means did not believe that there were any other substantive constraints upon management behaviour, this effectively left management more or less free to do exactly what they pleased.

Over the years the theory of the separation of ownership from control has become so much an accepted fact of life where analysis of the corporation is concerned that it is easy to forget just how little concrete evidence exists to support it. A typical comment on the subject is that by Galbraith [4] who asserts, without quoting any supporting evidence, that 'Among the two hundred largest corporations in the United States – those that form the heart of the industrial system – there are few in which owners exercise any important influence on decisions'.

The most substantive support for the theory comes from Larner who concluded his pilot study by suggesting [5] that 'it would appear that Berle and Means in 1929 were observing a "managerial revolution" in process. Now, thirty years later, that revolution seems close to complete, at least within the range of the 200 largest non-financial corporations'.

In a further study, this time of the 500 largest U.S. non-financial corporations in 1963,[6] Larner divided firms up into five categories, namely (1) those which were privately owned, (2) those controlled through the ownership of a majority (50–80 per cent) of the voting stock, (3) those controlled through the ownership of a dominant minority (10–15 per cent) of the voting stock, (4) those controlled by means of a legal device, and (5) those which were management controlled. He found that, whereas only five of the 500 firms investigated could be regarded as in private ownership, some 377 were under management control.[7]

These conclusions are not, however, beyond dispute. Sheehan [8] claimed, for example, that in 1967 controlling ownership of 150 of the

'Fortune 500' rested in the hands of an individual or of the members of a single family, where controlling ownership was defined as more than 10 per cent of the voting stock.

Villarejo [9] considered that a single interest of 5 per cent was generally sufficient for working control, and on that basis estimated [10] that one-half to three-fifths of the 250 largest U.S. industrial corporations in 1959 were owner controlled.[11] He therefore concluded that 'a relatively small group of persons, the propertied rich, both own and substantially control the giant enterprises of the nation'.[12]

Passing judgement on these various studies is difficult in the absence of a consistent interpretation of such terms as 'management control'. Beed [13] has made some interesting points in this context. He feels that Berle and Means never adequately proved their statement that [14] 'clearly no individual or small group was in a position to dominate the company through stock ownership'. Berle and Means looked at ownership registers in an attempt to determine whether or not there were any sufficiently large shareholder interests to dominate the company concerned in the legalistic sense. But as Beed points out,[15] the fact that one cannot detect a majority of shares registered in one person's name can be interpreted in two ways: 'either it could mean, with Berle and Means, that no one individual or small group could gain sufficient votes for control, *or*, contradicting Berle and Means, that only a few per cent of votes was required for control.' Beed quotes evidence gathered in Australia to indicate that a small number of minority interests of the order of 1 to 5 per cent of the voting shares could determine the structure of control, a figure below that considered necessary in the other studies referred to above.

It is as well to remember in addition that ultimate control over the way in which a voting share is exercised does not always lie in the hands of the individual in whose name the share is registered. By regrouping the largest shareholders and tracing their interrelationships, the over-all picture of minority share interests can change drastically.[16] Such relationships are often difficult to pin down, and care is frequently taken to cloud over the issue as to who precisely possesses voting rights. As a result, too much attention is sometimes paid to the problem of identifying in whose hands voting power resides, and too little paid to the other ways in which management behaviour is constrained, some of which are discussed below.

(ii) *The Role of Directors*

By law the ultimate source of control over the activities of a corporation is vested in its Board of Directors. It is therefore important to consider whether or not directors support the objectives of the shareholders who, in principle, elect them and to whom they are legally responsible, or whether they support the objectives of the management group.

Now the only two groups permitted to vote in an election of the Board of Directors are stockholders themselves or individuals to whom they have assigned their votes by proxy. In general, very few stockholders attend their firm's A.G.M., and it is customary for the firm's management to nominate a group of candidates agreeable to themselves, and to solicit proxy votes on behalf of these candidates. Most small stockholders either vote for the management's nominees *en masse* or do not bother to vote at all,[17] with the result that in most years the election of the Board of Directors is a foregone conclusion. In view of this it is commonly held that the Board of Directors is directly manipulated by the management group, and hence ceases to fulfil its proper role of protecting the interest of the stockholders.[18]

Since many directorships are regarded as a sinecure it would be rash to assume that directors can be relied upon to prevent management from pursuing objectives other than profit maximisation. On the other hand, it would be equally rash to suppose that management can operate without paying due regard to the interests of the stockholders, especially since it is relatively common for directors to hold shares in the firm on whose board they sit.[19] The standing of a firm is partly reflected by the presumed integrity of the members of its Board of Directors. Should well-known figures either be voted off or resign in protest against management policies it is probable that a proxy fight would develop. The evidence suggests, however, that such occasions are rare.[20] As Wildsmith has remarked: 'Perhaps equally interesting is the fact that so many managements are allowed to do so badly without being challenged',[21] an opinion shared by Larner who suggests that 'It seems improbable then, that close supervision by the Board of Directors imposes a tight curb on the exercise of managerial discretion.'[22]

In conclusion it is probably fair to say that the Board of Directors does operate as a constraint upon the freedom of management to pursue their own objectives, but that this constraint typically only comes into operation when the firm is doing particularly badly. As Larner has pointed out, the existence of the Board of Directors can be accommodated by a slight amendment to the meaning of management control.[23] 'Management control then, simply means that the management in the absence of gross incompetence or serious misfortune, has open to it a wide range of discretionary behaviour in which it can, without fear of punitive action by stockholders pursue policies which serve its own interests at the expense of the owners.[24]

(iii) *Take-over Bids*

Another factor dismissed by Berle and Means as unlikely to act as a constraint upon management behaviour is the implied threat of a take-over bid if a firm's performance is consistently below par. The contrary opinion is however voiced by Tullock,[25] Hindley,[26] and Manne,[27] and to a lesser extent Marris,[28] who argues that the odds against being taken over are rather low.

Specific evidence on this issue is extremely sparse at present, and the case for supporting the view that threat of take-over is likely to cause management to adhere fairly closely to profit-maximising behaviour rests in good part upon the general evidence of the flurry of merger activity over the past two decades. But there is no evidence to suggest that the probability that an unprofitable firm will be taken over is significantly greater than the probability for a relatively profitable firm.[29] Furthermore, it is a relatively well-known fact that widespread replacement of the management of a taken-over firm does not in any way guarantee a subsequent improvement in performance, and managers may well console themselves with the thought that they are too valuable to be dismissed. Fear of dismissal as a direct consequence of a successful take-over bid is therefore unlikely to loom large as a factor determining management behaviour.

(iv) *Outside Capital*

One extreme view concerning the impact of outside capital upon management behaviour is to the effect that 'major corporations in most instances do not seek capital. They form it themselves'.[30] If this is true then it clearly frees corporations from the constraint of scrutiny by bodies from whom outside capital has to be raised. Dooley, however, points out[31] that in the United States 'the total liabilities of non-financial business approach one half trillion dollars, that about one third of the assets of the 100 largest non-financial corporations are financed on credit, and that these 100 corporations interlock (directors) 616 times with the fifty largest banks and life insurance companies alone'. On this evidence he concludes that management is subject to pressure from external sources of finance. This view is shared by Chevalier,[32] but Beed[33] and Hindley[34] are less sure. Hindley points out, for example, that the need to raise new capital will enter into managerial calculations 'only in so far as the managers wish to achieve objectives for which the flow of capital available from retained earnings or the issue of bonds will not suffice'.

Once again this is not an issue on which it is possible to draw strong conclusions at the present time. There is, on the whole, much to be said for Wildsmith's tentative opinion[35] that 'the capital market cannot be ignored: indeed there is a strong suggestion that manager's attitude to shareholders is much more positive than the term "constraint" would imply.' Support for this opinion can also be found in the discussion of management shareholdings in the section below.

(v) *Management Shareholdings*

It is evident that managers who have extensive shareholdings in their own firms will want to protect their interests by ensuring that profits are not sacrificed unnecessarily through the pursuit of objectives which maximise the satisfaction of managers rather than that of shareholders.[36]

It is interesting to note that the absence of any meaningful distinction between ownership and control is a basic tenet of the Marxist interpretation of modern capitalism. Baran and Sweezy, for example, point out that[37]

> there is no justification for concluding from (the apparent freedom of management from stockholder control) that managements in general are divorced from ownership in general. Quite the contrary, managers are among the biggest owners; and because of the strategic positions they occupy they function as the protectors and spokesmen for all large scale property. Far from being a separate class, they constitute in reality the leading echelon of the property owning class.

Evidence confirming the existence of large management shareholdings in their own firms also comes from commentators of less-extreme political persuasions. Villarejo,[38] for example, states that 'One group of shareholders enjoying an especially rapid expansion of ownership has been the corporate executives or "top management".' Likewise Larner[39] considers that 'Although the largest single component of executive compensation is still salary and bonus, we have seen that deferred and contingent forms of compensation, and particularly stock options, having been increasing in relative importance and by 1963 were nearly as large as salary and bonus in the compensation package of top executives.'

The practice of rewarding top management with stock options is certainly much more common in the United States (to which the above evidence relates) than in the United Kingdom, although the relatively penal rates of tax on earned incomes in the United Kingdom have tended to make stock options an increasingly attractive way to receive appropriate rewards for good management.

(vi) *Implications for Managerial Behaviour*

It is important to bear in mind that it is one thing to argue that control over the modern corporation has passed from shareholders to managers, but quite another to contend that this will have significant implications for managerial behaviour.

We may note at the outset that the evidence relating to the independence of management from outside control is by no means conclusive. One of the major difficulties in this context has been aptly summarised by Beed, who points out that[40] 'passive control may never exhibit itself in an active manner. That such exhibition is lacking does not disprove its existence, but quantification of it becomes impossible.' The same point is emphasised by Villarejo, who asks,[41] 'Why exercise a controlling position when management is doing a good job?'

But even if it is accepted that, in principle, management need pay but lip-service to the wishes of outside interests they may, in practice, prove to be a good deal more accommodating. In Sheehan's view[42] 'very few executives agree that the managers of a widely held company run their business any differently from the proprietors of a closely held company. Competition is a great leveller and both managers and proprietors respond to its pressures with equal spirit and objectivity.'

Acceptance of this viewpoint necessarily diminishes the importance of the long-standing controversy concerning the separation of ownership and control, a point not lost on Larner who concludes his study thus:[43]

On the basis of the evidence presently available, I conclude that, although control is separated from ownership in most of America's largest corporations, the effects in the profit orientation of firms and on stockholders' welfare have been minor. [Some empirical evidence on the relative profitability of owner-controlled and management-controlled firms is set out on pp. 121–2.] The magnitude of the effects appears to be too small to justify the considerable attention they have received in the literature for the past 38 years.

Finally we may take note of an article by De Alessi[44] which takes to task more or less everyone who has written about this controversy. In his opinion

Whatever else these and similar studies may do they provide no evidence whatsoever on management control for any non-trivial definition of the term. If a given profile of share distribution is to reflect management control, then the activities of the firm must differ in some observable way from the activities that would have occurred under an alternative profile, say one reflecting stockholders' control . . . The empirical evidence so far does not provide a definitive test of the hypothesis that different degrees of dispersion imply different outcomes to the firm's decision process.[45]

Chapter 16

Sales-Revenue Maximisation

Baumol [1] has put forward the idea that a firm has as its objective the maximisation of sales revenue subject to a profit constraint. He claimed that firms give precedence to the pursuit of maximum sales revenue over the pursuit of maximum profit because managers believe that their salaries, power and standing, both within their own company and within the business community at large, are more closely related to the attainment of the former than the latter objective.

(i) *The Sales-Revenue-Maximisation Model*

Now the objective of maximum sales revenue clearly requires that ownership be separate from control. Nevertheless, management can never be wholly free from shareholder influence. They must at all times earn sufficient profits to enable the firm to pay out dividends large enough to keep shareholders in a contented state. Hence Baumol postulated the existence of a profit constraint.

Now profit is equivalent to the difference between revenue and cost. Hence we can derive the total-profit curve as illustrated in Figure 16.1 by taking the vertical distance between the total-revenue and total-cost curve at each level of output and measuring the same distance up from the horizontal axis. No profits are earned on any output either less than OA or greater than OD because profits are only earned where revenues exceed costs. *Profits* are *maximised* where the two curves are furthest apart, which is at output OB. On the other hand, *sales revenue* will be *maximised* at the highest point on the total-revenue curve indicated by output OE.

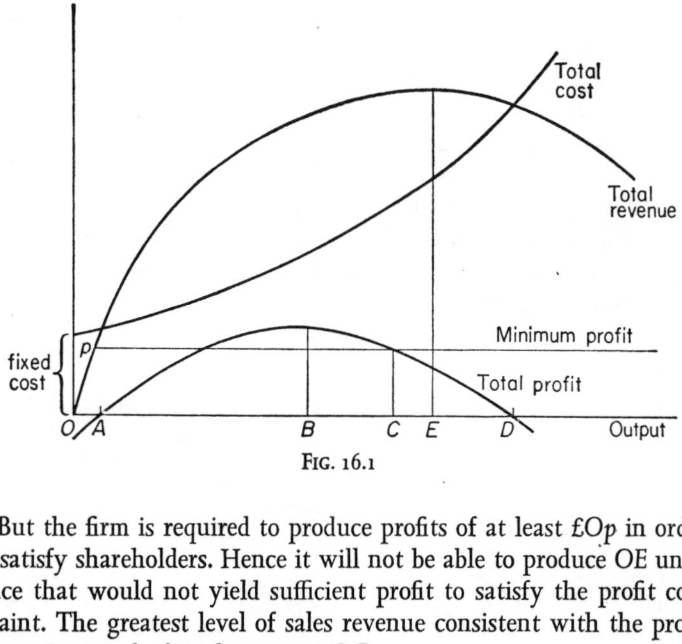

FIG. 16.1

But the firm is required to produce profits of at least £O*p* in order to satisfy shareholders. Hence it will not be able to produce OE units since that would not yield sufficient profit to satisfy the profit constraint. The greatest level of sales revenue consistent with the profit constraint is to be found at output OC.

The precise magnitude of the profit constraint is, however, left rather vague. In Baumol's model it refers to a level of profit high enough both to keep existing shareholders happy and to make the firm an attractive prospect to would-be shareholders. However, the vagueness of this definition makes it difficult to specify the firm's optimal output with any precision.

(ii) *The Role of Advertising*

On the other hand, this theory does have the advantage that it can be extended to make allowance for the significant role typically played by advertising in a large corporation. Where a firm expands its sales by cutting its prices it may, or may not, achieve an increase in revenue, depending upon the elasticity of demand for the product. But where a firm expands its sales by virtue of an increase in its advertising expenditures it must always increase its revenues since price per unit sold remains unchanged whereas output has risen (thus yielding a total-revenue curve which rises constantly but at a diminishing rate). This can be seen in Figure 16.2 where the horizontal axis now measures outlays on advertising and the total-cost curve includes expenditures on advertising. The profits curve is once again derived by taking the difference between total revenue and total cost, and we can see that the level of advertising outlays which would maximise profits is equal to *OB*. Where, however, the firm is seeking to maximise sales revenue subject to a profit constraint of *Op* it will spend OA on advertising. This may reasonably be regarded as somewhat excessive since it exceeds the expenditure on advertising undertaken by a profit-maximising firm.

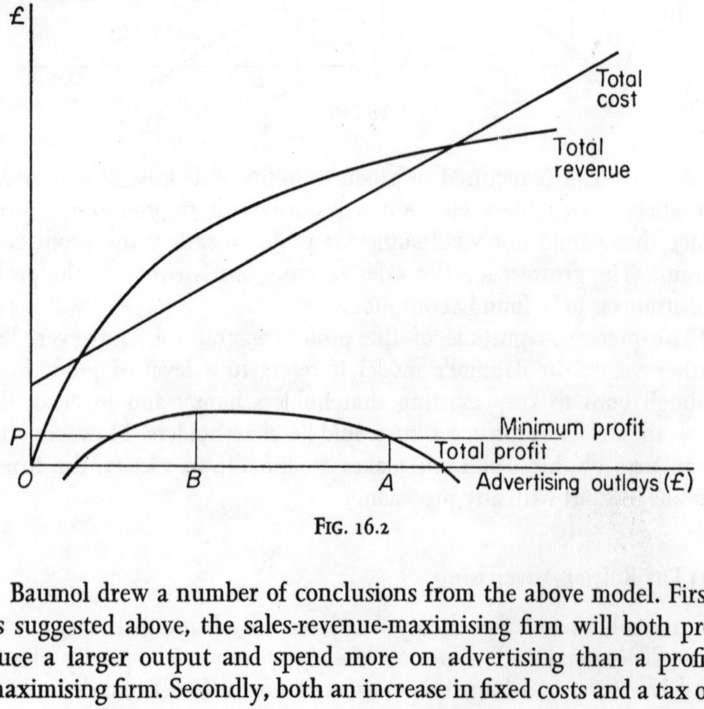

FIG. 16.2

Baumol drew a number of conclusions from the above model. First, as suggested above, the sales-revenue-maximising firm will both produce a larger output and spend more on advertising than a profit-maximising firm. Secondly, both an increase in fixed costs and a tax on profits prior to their distribution in the form of dividends will force the sales-revenue-maximising firm to reduce output and raise price, since it will no longer be possible for the firm to meet its profit constraint at its existing output level. A profit-maximising firm's price and output will, however, remain unchanged in such circumstances since neither the marginal-cost nor marginal-revenue curves will have shifted their positions.

(iii) *Criticisms of the Model*

The Baumol model has been subjected to widespread criticism. On a theoretical level Shepherd [2] has suggested that under conditions of oligopoly the kinked demand curve model would apply, in which case, depending upon the extent of the kink, revenues and profits could be simultaneously maximised. Hence 'the more there is of oligopolistic interdependence, the less will sales-maximisation affect or explain output decisions'.

Other attempts have been made to demonstrate that the sales-revenue-maximisation and profit-maximisation objectives produce the same price–output combination in the long run. Mabry and Siders [3] set out to test Baumol's contention that firms attempt to maximise sales revenue even at the expense of higher profits, taking for examination the period 1952–63 in the United States. They found that firms with greater changes in sales also tended to have greater changes in profits, which was taken to suggest that the sales-revenue-maximisation hypothesis and the profit-maximisation hypothesis are consistent in the long run. This finding is confirmed by Mabry [4] who also uses the kinked demand curve model to demonstrate the feasible consistency of the two hypotheses in the short run.

Hawkins concludes, however,[5] that 'wherever advertising and/or other non-price forms of competition are possible (almost everywhere in oligopoly?) the sales revenue maximiser will choose to produce a greater output and, in order to gain demand for it, will advertise more than the profit maximiser. Both firms will choose the same price.' Hence the sales-revenue maximiser and profit maximiser only choose the same output where 'advertising and all other forms of non-price competition are either completely ineffective or impossible'. On the other hand, he suggests elsewhere that [6] 'it can be shown that revenue maximisers need not necessarily produce more output and advertise more than profit maximisers. They may produce less output (with higher advertising and a higher price). Equally they may advertise *less* than profit maximisers (with a higher output and a lower price)'

On a more general level Alchian [7] has pointed out that the model is open to the objection 'that it implies the firm will not make any sacrifice in sales, no matter how large an increment in wealth would thereby be achievable'.

(iv) *The Empirical Evidence*

One obvious test of the validity of the above model is to produce evidence in support of the proposition that 'Executive salaries appear to be far more closely correlated with the scale of operations of the firm than with its profitability.' [8] Patton concluded [9] that executive pay is directly related to company size, and that above-average pay leads to above-average profits. Similarly, Roberts found [10] that the relationship between executive pay and sales was apparently stronger than that between pay and profits. Chiu, Elbing,[11] and McGuire investigated the correlations between executive incomes, sales and profits for 45 of the largest 100 corporations in the United States from 1953 to 1959. They found that 'the line of apparent causation runs from sales to incomes rather than incomes to sales', and that 'Executive compensation is primarily a reward for past sales results.'

Hall, however,[12] hypothesising that 'positive departures from the profit constraint should set in motion forces that will lead to increases in sales revenue' found no evidence to support this supposition.[13] Mabry [14] suggested that 'a higher correlation between executive incomes and sales than between income and profits does not imply that executives seek to maximise sales rather than profits'. This is because 'There is strong reason to believe that biased forces in the forms of executive compensation produce this result. Upon analysis the validity of the correlations and the conclusions drawn from them are open to question.'

Masson, furthermore, finds the studies purporting to support the Baumol hypothesis wholly unpalatable,[15] particularly the way in which they ignore executive ownership of stock in their own companies.[16] Llewellen [17] had previously estimated that the ratio of compensation based on executive stock and stock options to other compensation was of the order of five to one. Hence Masson feels that

Executive financial incentives are found to be primarily related to firm stock market performance. The sales performance of the firm has no consistent positive or negative effect on executive financial return. . . . It was found that firms with executives whose financial rewards more closely paralleled stockholders' interests performed better in the stock market over the post-war period.

This opinion is shared by Larner, who concludes that [18] 'The results suggest that the corporation's dollar profit and rate of profit are the major variables explaining the level of executive remuneration and compensation.' It is difficult, therefore, to arrive at a definite conclusion as to the validity of the sales-revenue-maximisation model.

Chapter 17

Growth Models

(i) *The Models Compared*

A number of models have been developed which stress the objective of growth. One of these had its origins in Baumol's dissatisfaction with his static sales-revenue-maximisation model,[1] to which he made two main modifications.

First maximisation of *rate of growth* of sales revenue seems a somewhat better approximation to the goals of many management groups in large firms than is maximisation of the current *level* of sales.

The second modification deals with the nature of the profit constraint which in a static model may have seemed to be arbitrarily imposed from the outside. In the later model the profit constraint becomes the 'means for obtaining capital needed to finance expansion plans'. But beyond some point profits compete with sales. Thus 'the optimal profit stream' will be that intermediate stream which is consistent with the largest flow of output (or rate of growth of output) over the firm's lifetime.

This model was extended by J. H. Williamson,[2] who came down strongly in favour of the growth-maximising hypothesis subject to the amendment that 'growth is never limited by lack of finance as such . . . but by the fear of takeover'. According to his calculations a profit maximiser would choose the same output level as a growth maximiser whereas a sales-revenue maximiser would produce a larger output. Additionally, 'A profit or growth maximizer will grow at a positive rate if it is a profitable firm; a sales maximizer need not', and 'A profit maximizer would, except in a limiting case, distribute more of its profits than a growth maximizer.'

The most extensive work on growth models is that done by Marris,[3] who takes as his starting point the separation of ownership from control. He develops a model based on the hypothesis that managers are primarily concerned with the growth rate of their firms subject to a minimum constraint on security.[4] He points out that if managers were concerned simply with size *per se* they would move from small firms to larger firms and subsequently to even larger firms. However, most managers prefer to stay put in their existing firms. Consequently, 'managements are likely to see the growth of their own organization as one of the best methods for satisfying personal needs and ambitions'.[5] Salary, power and prestige result from policies of rapid growth, so the manager is motivated to pursue such policies. Growth and security are, however, competing objectives, since the pursuit of security demands conservative financial policies such as excess liquidity, whereas growth requires the undertaking of relatively risky investments and risky methods of obtaining capital.

In particular, security is sought from the threat of take-over which Marris considers will tend to become more likely where the firm has

(I) an internal rate of return on productive assets substantially lower than could be obtained with a complete change of management;

(II) an excessive retention ratio, especially but not only in firms suffering from (I) with little prospect of early change;

(III) excessive liquidity.

On the other hand, he points out that 'A minimum-profit restraint inhibits the firm's ability to stimulate growth of demand for its products while a restraint on retentions affects its ability to obtain capital to meet the demand.' Thus he suggests that it is possible to envisage a trade-off relationship between growth and security. This relationship will be such that the extent of the trade-off cannot be altered in favour of shareholders. 'The best the shareholders can get is the position of over-all optimum for the managers, since the managers in choosing this point, take just that much account of the stockholders' bargaining position that they, the managers, regard as optimal.'[6]

One consequence of successful growth maximisation is a greater share of the market. However, total concentration is avoided 'because the most successful maximisers of today are not the most successful tomorrow'. In practice, Marris considers that his theory predicts accurately the existing size distribution of industry.[7]

(ii) *Criticisms of the Models*

The Marris model has been subjected to considerable criticism. One line of attack is typified by Solow,[8] who argued that first,

> the alternative theory – that corporations maximize long-run profits, more or less, and expand whenever they earn more than a target rate of return – also entails that successful companies will be growing most of the time, and will no doubt be talking about it, and secondly that devotion to growth is quite consistent with profit maximization if profit is interpreted as the after-tax return to the stockholder because long-term capital gains are not taxed as heavily as dividends.

Mueller pointed out[9] that the problem with the growth hypothesis was not its theoretical justification but 'the failure of both its defenders and its critics to recognise that its validity probably varies depending on the age of the firm and its investment opportunities'. He began by postulating the separation of ownership from control and went on to argue that managers' non-pecuniary rewards are 'directly associated with size and growth and not with profitability'. For this reason, even though a growing firm will be subject eventually to managerial diseconomies of scale and a declining rate of return on its investments, managers' pursuit of growth is not limited by a desire to maximise shareholder welfare but by limited availability of investment funds, threat of take-over and compassion for stockholders. Mueller thus expected a growth-maximising firm to 'undertake more investment than a stockholder-welfare maximiser, pay equivalently smaller dividends, grow at a faster rate, and have a lower market value for its firm'.

Mueller also expected, however, that the freedom to pursue growth and the accompanying conflict between owners and managers would only appear over time as a firm expanded and matured. 'At the firm's creation the stockholders have complete control over the amount of investment undertaken since they supply all of the initial capital.' Over time the capital shortage disappears, first because its internal-fund flows eventually outpace its new investment opportunities, and secondly because the reduction in uncertainty regarding the future following its early success lowers the cost of outside capital. Gradually, however, managers' interests supersede those of the stockholders who are powerless to prevent this happening.

After surveying the literature [10] Mueller could find no direct evidence to support the growth-maximisation hypothesis. On the other hand, he detected favourable evidence to the extent that 'the returns mature firms earned by reinvesting their internal cash flows appear to be substantially below their stockholders' outside investment opportunities'.[11]

A final line of attack is contained in the argument that growth models have so far needed to be grossly over-simplified in order to make them manageable.[12] Whether or not this objection will eventually be overcome is a matter of some debate.

(iii) *The Empirical Evidence*

Marris's model provides us with a testable hypothesis because it follows from the above discussion that owner-controlled firms should, on average, achieve lower growth rates and higher profit rates than management-controlled firms. Radice,[13] for example, set out to test this hypothesis with respect to eighty-nine firms in the food, electrical engineering, and textile industries in the United Kingdom for the period 1957–67. For the purposes of his study 'companies in which there was a definable interest group holding more than 15% of the voting shares were classified as owner-controlled and where the proportion was less than 5% as management-controlled'.[14] He concluded that

> differences in performance do appear to exist between the two control types in profitability. But whereas we might have expected the higher profit rates of owner-controlled firms to be associated with lower growth rates than those of management-controlled firms the former are in fact superior in both respects. In addition they show greater variability in the relationship between profit and growth rates.

The evidence is confirmed by Monsen, Chiu and Cooley, who conclude that [15]

An analysis of the data reveals that the owner-controlled group of firms outperformed the management-controlled firms by a considerable margin. The net income to net worth ratio was 75% higher for owner-controlled firms than the management-controlled ones over the twelve-year period. This result indicates that the owner-controlled firm provides a much better return on the original investment and suggests a better managed capital structure and more efficient allocation of the owners' resources.

On the other hand Kamerschen [16] is of the opinion that the type of control does not appear to explain very much of the variation in profit rates among the 200 largest non-financial companies included in the study by Larner.[17] Hindley [18] also considers that the control status of firms does not crucially affect firm performance, a view which is shared by Llewellen,[19] who sees no great point in trying to separate out the various pecuniary interests of ownership and management in view of the evidence of extensive shareholdings of executives in their own companies.

Chapter 18

Biological Theories of the Firm

A number of theories of the firm have their roots in the physical sciences, particularly in biology. Such theories can be divided into two groups consisting of (1) theories of *homeostasis* which emphasise short-run changes, and (2) theories of *viability* which emphasise long-run changes.[1] In both cases the underlying analogy is that firms, like organisms, start small, then mature and produce offspring, and eventually die.

(i) *Homeostasis*

Homeostasis is a synonym for stability. It is alleged that physical organisms always attempt to lead stable lives [2] because change is threatening and requires the organism to go to great lengths to adapt to its changed circumstances. Boulding has suggested [3] that 'there is some "state" of the organism which it is organised to maintain, and any disturbance from this state sets in motion behaviour on the part of the organism which tends to re-establish the desired state'. In Boulding's scheme the notion of equilibrium is more general than that of maximisation, although there will always be some firms seeking to maximise profits even where most other firms are pursuing what Boulding calls 'the line of least resistance'.

Now where a firm pursues the objective of homeostasis it requires only to decide upon a set of norms for its behaviour. Once these norms have been established any deviation from them automatically sets up forces within the firm which correct the deviations and re-establish the norm. The original set of norms may either be unique to the individual firm or may be borrowed from another firm which is considered to have achieved great success. The set of norms may thus come in a variety of guises. Typically, however, it involves a fixed relationship between some of the variables to be found in the firm's balance sheet or between costs and price (see pp. 91–3). Where, however, a firm employs any kind of inflexible relationship between operating variables it is unlikely that the end result will be profit maximisation since this latter objective requires that a firm continuously varies its operating procedures in order to take advantage of even small changes in market conditions.

(ii) *Viability*

Alchian's suggested approach [4] embodies 'the principles of biological evolution and natural selection by interpreting the economic system as an adaptive mechanism which chooses among exploratory actions generated by the adaptive pursuit of "success" or "profits" '. He begins by accepting Tintner's postulate [5] that, in an uncertain world, profit maximisation is a meaningless guide to specifiable action because he feels that realised positive profits, not maximum profits are the mark of success and viability. Furthermore, 'it does not matter through what process of reasoning or motivation such success was achieved. The fact of its accomplishment is sufficient'.

Now, 'positive profits accrue to those who are better than their actual competitors' irrespective of how good or bad those competitors may be. Also, 'the greater the uncertainties of the world the greater is the possibility that profits would go to venturesome and lucky rather than to logical, careful, fact-gathering individuals'. This suggests that relatively superior firms survive, but also that it is as much a matter of luck as of good judgement as to which firms happen to be relatively superior at any given point in time.

It is customarily assumed that surviving firms must have adapted themselves to their environment. On the other hand, there may have been no motivated adapting, in which case surviving firms must have been adopted by their environment. For this reason Alchian does not regard the survival of certain firms over long periods of time as *prima facie* proof of their adaptability. He considers that one needs to know how many firms started off together and the size, risk and frequency of each commitment. Thus, rather than there being 'too many firms with long lives in the real world to admit an important role to chance . . . one might insist that there are actually too few'.[6]

Two forms of adaptive behaviour are, however, emphasised. First, firms tend to imitate the successful behaviour of other firms. This, Alchian claims, has led to the widespread introduction of conventional mark-ups, price leadership, accounting ratios, and so forth. In an uncertain world imitation appears less risky than the introduction of untried concepts. Imitative behaviour cannot, however, guarantee success, which often requires the willingness to abandon such behaviour when the time is ripe.

Secondly, firms can adapt through a process of trial and error, selecting those policies which appear to have moved the firm to some extent nearer to its optimal operating position. This is, however, a short-term process since a firm cannot in a world of uncertainty foresee the whole sequence of policies which will eventually lead to profit maximisation.

Firms are therefore regarded as relatively passive. However, despite this lack of motivation many firms are adopted by the environment and survive. Other firms are able to adapt successfully through imitation or trial and error, but here again long-run survival requires that they are relatively lucky in moving away from established patterns of behaviour at exactly the right time.

Biological analogies of this kind have been severely criticised. For example, Penrose[7] points out that 'the development of firms does not proceed according to the same "grim" laws as does that of living organisms', and also that to abandon the development of firms to 'the laws of nature' diverts attention from the importance of human decisions and motives and from problems of ethics and public policy, and surrounds the whole question of the growth of the firm with an aura of 'naturalness' and even 'inevitability'. She feels that mankind, unlike other species, has the ability to adapt his environment to suit himself, or to become independent of it, whereas biological theories allow only that man can adapt to his environment. Thus she feels that any analogy which passes over the ability of an organism to consciously deliberate should be discarded.

Chapter 19

Utility Maximisation

(i) *Introduction*

The term 'utility maximisation' is customarily applied to those models which hypothesise that managers set out to maximise their own utility rather than that of shareholders. Whereas shareholders are supposed to derive utility almost exclusively from profits, managers may derive utility from pursuing a whole range of possible objectives. Most obviously, managers can attempt to maximise their monetary rewards. Alternatively, they can set out to increase their leisure time and to make their lives generally as easy as possible. In so far as the term 'utility' is, in practice, more than a little vague it is possible to argue that any non-profit-maximising theory of the firm is a utility-maximising model. It is customary, however, to restrict the usage of the term to exclude, for example, the model of sales-revenue maximisation.

The inclusion of the various models which follow under the heading of utility-maximising models is, therefore, somewhat arbitrary. Furthermore, there is necessarily a considerable overlap with the theories of satisficing behaviour which appear in the following chapter since, irrespective of the objectives of the managerial group, the need to earn sufficient profits to keep the shareholders happy cannot be ignored.

The best-specified utility-maximising model is probably that of

Williamson (see pp. 130–1). As we shall discover, however, all utility-maximising models necessarily suffer from a lack of generality. This results largely from the fact that managers are individuals and tend not to put equal value upon, for example, monetary versus non-monetary rewards, or upon income versus leisure. The trade-off between income and leisure forms the basis of the section below. We follow this with a résumé of Papandreou's concept of a 'preference function' and subsequently with a discussion of the proposal that managers set out to maximise their life-time incomes. The last two sections comprise (1) an examination of Williamson's 'expense preference' model, and (2) a summary of the not-dissimilar 'X-theory of the firm'.

Unlike most other theories expounded in this book utility-maximisation models have rarely been empirically tested. One suspects that this is due in large part to the difficulty of restricting to manageable proportions the number of variables yielding utility in the model while still producing predictions with a high degree of generality. Whatever the truth of the matter one must conclude that, although in principle utility maximisation holds out the prospect of a plausible alternative to profit maximisation, since it essentially proposes that managers do what is best for themselves, there is no prospect, in practice, of such a model with any worthwhile degree of generality appearing in the near future.

(ii) *Income versus Leisure*

Hicks [1] has stated that 'the best of all monopoly profits is a quiet life', and this suggestion has subsequently been incorporated into theories of business behaviour proposed by Scitovsky,[2] Nettl,[3] and Reder.[4] Managers are assumed to be continuously faced by a choice between more profit and more leisure. In general, managers find the attractions of more leisure growing stronger as the firm's profits rise, and it is suggested that, in practice, managers do not always work hard enough to maximise profits, which would only happen where a manager's desire for greater profits is unaffected by the level of profits so far earned. Regrettably no evidence as to the frequency with which this occurs is currently available. Once again it would seem to depend a good deal upon the extent of the separation of ownership from control, although there is considerable controversy [5] as to whether it is the entrepreneur or the salaried manager who is the more likely to forgo profits in favour of an easier life. The entrepreneur stands to gain more personally if profits are maximised. On the other hand, a manager's income is not so readily substitutable with leisure.

(iii) *Maximisation of a Preference Function*

Some of the early work on managerial discretion was done by Papandreou,[6] who introduces the concept of the maximisation of a preference function. He conceives of a 'peak co-ordinator' who formulates the firm's operating budget or strategy. The selection of strategy requires the specification of some value premises (preference system) and factual premises. The preference system is 'regarded as being a resultant of all the influences which affect the value premises of enterprise strategy selection'.[7] Over a period of time the peak co-ordinator is subject to a 'changing structure of conscious influence' which largely arises out of the separation of ownership from control and from the rise of the trade unions.

The firm is thus taken to be seeking the maximisation of its general preference function rather than of profits. The sort of factors which tend to enter a firm's preference function are the desires for 'a quiet life', for power, for control, or for prestige. But, as Papendreou himself points out, the difficulties of quantifying a preference function are considerable so that 'we must always take pains to impart empirical meaningfulness to our model'.[8]

(iv) *Maximisation of Lifetime Income*

A fairly extreme view of the effects of managerial discretion is that postulated by Monsen and Downs, who suggest that, whereas owners seek maximum profits managers 'act so as to maximise their own lifetime incomes'.[9] Stockholders are, in general, considered unlikely to switch from holding shares in one company to holding them in another because of uncertainty about the outcome of the switch and because capital gains are taxed. Thus they tend to accept 'satisfactory' profit levels without much fuss. On the one hand, managers are aware of the possibility of an uprising among shareholders if they perform particularly badly but, on the other hand, managers do not expect optimum performance to be commensurately rewarded. Hence 'the punishment for grievous error is greater than the reward for outstanding success'.[10] Thus, subject to the need to earn satisfactory profits for shareholders, managers seek to maximise 'the present value of their lifetime incomes in dollar terms' (where such incomes include both monetary and non-monetary elements). Unfortunately no empirical justification of their theory is provided, and the model appears inferior to that of Williamson which is discussed below.

(v) *Expense Preference*

A comprehensive model of managerial discretion has been developed by Williamson.[11] At the heart of his model is the concept of *expense preference*. 'That is the management does not have a neutral attitude towards costs. Directly or indirectly certain classes of expenditure have positive values associated with them. In particular staff expense expenditure for emoluments, and funds available for discretionary investment have value additional to that which derives from their productivity.'[12] Staff expansion is particularly hard to resist because 'not only is it an indirect means to the attainment of salary but it is also a source of security, power, status, prestige and professional achievement as well'. By 'emoluments' Williamson means discretionary pay and perquisites which are in excess of what needs to be offered in order to retain a manager's services, and which therefore constitute part of organisational slack as defined below (see pp. 45–7). This slack may either be attained by way of additional salary or by way of non-pecuniary perquisites since, in the latter case, there is much less likelihood of giving offence to either shareholders or workers.

However, 'the existence of satisfactory profits is necessary to assure the interference-free operation of the firm to the management'. Furthermore, management 'will find it desirable to earn profits that exceed the acceptable level. For one thing managers derive satisfaction from self-fulfilment and organizational achievement and profits are one measure of this success. In addition profits are a source of discretion'.[13] Williamson then combines the various managerial goals into a *utility function* and postulates that the objective of *utility maximisation* will override that of profit maximisation.

The utility-maximisation and profit-maximisation models can be compared and contrasted by considering the effects of the imposition of various taxes upon the two models. A profit-maximising firm is unaffected by the imposition of either a profits tax or a lump-sum tax, since in neither case can it pass on the tax to its customers. Furthermore, there is, by definition, no available slack which the profit-maximising firm can eliminate in order to boost profits.

However, the imposition of a profits tax constitutes a penalty imposed upon reported profits, to which a utility-maximising firm can be expected to respond by transforming part of what would otherwise have been reported profit into organisational slack of various kinds. Furthermore, in the case of a lump-sum tax this raises the quantity of pre-tax profits which a utility-maximising firm must generate in order to meet its minimum post-tax profit constraint. Hence such a firm must undertake to raise its pre-tax profits by eliminating some source of organisational slack. This implies that, unlike a profit-maximising firm whose price–output combination is unaffected in the short run by a change in fixed costs (in which category a lump-sum tax can reasonably be included), a utility-maximising firm will have to modify its behaviour in order to meet its minimum profit constraint.

Finally, we may note that both profit-maximising and utility-maximising firms can be expected to expand output and take on more staff when demand is expanding, and to curtail output and fire staff when demand is on the decline. The difference between the two types of firm is, however, that, whereas a profit-maximising firm never develops slack, a utility-maximising firm will incur additional slack in boom periods and will seek ways of eliminating it when the going gets bad.

Williamson provides empirical evidence based upon field studies and statistical analysis to support his hypothesis that 'those expenditures that promote managerial satisfactions should show a positive correlation with opportunities for discretion and tastes'.[14] His conclusion was that the evidence

> generally supports the implications of the utility-maximization approach. Although it is not strong enough to provide a discrimination between the utility and profits-maximizing theories, it does suggest that either firms are operated as indicated by the managerial model, or, if 'actual' profits are maximized, that reported profits are reduced by absorbing some fraction of actual profits in executive salaries and possibly in perquisites of a variety of sorts.

(vi) X-*inefficiency*

For a long period after the war surprisingly little attention was paid to the question of cost efficiency. It was well known that a firm in a perfectly competitive market needed to produce as cheaply as its competitors if it wished to survive, since at the prevailing price level even normal profits could be earned in the long run only where a firm held its costs down to a bare minimum. Furthermore, profit maximisation necessarily implied cost minimisation, so that any firm pursuing the objective of maximum profits was automatically assumed to be undertaking whatever were the appropriate courses of action in order to keep costs at their lowest possible level. Hence acknowledgement of the oligopolistic nature of most industrial markets did not affect the assumption of cost efficiency *per se*, and even the development of alternative objectives to that of profit maximisation was not allowed to disturb the inviolacy of this assumption.

In 1966, however, a seminal paper by Leibenstein entitled 'Allocative Efficiency versus X-Efficiency',[15] brought into focus the validity of the cost-efficiency assumption. Leibenstein introduced the concept of X-*inefficiency* which he defined as the difference between the lowest level of costs potentially achievable and the level of costs actually being achieved. He blamed the onset of X-inefficiency upon a number of factors, principal amongst them being the lack of knowledge possessed by a firm with respect to the optimum combinations of factor inputs, and also the propensity of labour inputs at all levels in the hierarchy to work at less than their full capacity (which he referred to in the case of management as 'intellectual slack'). He concluded that[16]

> for a variety of reasons people and organizations work neither as hard nor as effectively as they could. In situations where competitive pressure is light many people will trade the disutility of greater effort, of search, and the control of other people's activities for the utility of feeling less pressure and of better inter-personal relations, but in situations where competitive pressures are high, and hence the costs of such trades are also high, they will exchange less of the disutility of effort for the utility of freedom from pressure. . . . The data suggests that in a great many instances the amount to be gained by increasing X-efficiency is frequently significant.

Leibenstein went on to suggest that X-inefficiency would increase in line with increases in a firm's monopoly power. This is intuitively plausible since a perfectly competitive firm must be wholly X-efficient whereas monopoly power greatly reduces the extent of competition, and hence allows a firm to become increasingly inefficient without in the process losing more than a marginal share of its market to its rivals. The precise nature of the relationship between X-inefficiency and the degree of competition was not, however, specified by Leibenstein in his paper, and attempts to rectify this omission have developed into the *X-theory of the firm.*[17]

The X-theory of the firm presupposes the existence of the separation of ownership from control (see pp. 103–5). This implies that there is continuing conflict between the shareholders who want management to pursue the objective of profit maximisation, and management themselves who wish to pursue objectives of their own choosing, for example growth, sales maximisation or leisure. In the absence of stringent controls imposed by the shareholders, X-inefficiency will inevitably creep in, but its incidence will be constrained in a number of ways. Most important of all will be monetary incentives to promote co-operation from both management and workers, quite possibly linked in some way to current profit levels,[18] and the introduction of regulatory devices designed to ensure that the requisite effort is being made by employees at all levels in the firm's hierarchy.

In the latter case, however, there is a cost involved in the setting up and running of an efficacious system of controls, and there must come a point where it costs more to impose further controls than could potentially be saved by way of a reduction in X-inefficiency brought about by such controls.[19] It is not, therefore, realistic to expect a wholesale elimination of X-inefficiency, and even if this could be achieved the resultant level of costs would be higher than that pertaining in an equivalent but perfectly competitive industry because allowance would have to be made for the cost of the system of regulatory controls.

The existence of X-inefficiency in large corporations is undoubtedly very pervasive although there have not as yet been many attempts to assess directly its importance in individual firms. The evidence quoted in Leibenstein's original paper is itself to some extent suspect because he failed to make proper allowance for the role played by economies of scale in accounting for differences in costs as between firms. However, it is supported by case-study material quoted as the basis for the development of alternative theories of the firm [20] which, although they introduce their own terminology such as 'satisficing behaviour' and 'organisational slack', essentially make the same points as have been made above.

Elsewhere Rowley [21] has demonstrated a close relationship between the level of X-inefficiency and the degree of monopoly power in both the U.K. and U.S. steel industries, and Leibenstein [22] has used evidence cited in Mansfield [23] to suggest that X-inefficiency accounts for the long time lags which have occurred between many inventions and their adoption, and also for the slow spread of technological innovations.

Chapter 20

Theories of Satisficing Behaviour

(i) *Satisficing Theory*

We have already referred on several occasions to the need for a firm to earn sufficient profits in order to satisfy its shareholders. In those cases we regarded satisfactory profits as an objective which ran alongside, but which was subsidiary to, other objectives. There are, however, a number of theories which regard the achievement of satisfactory profits as the firm's primary objective, this objective replacing that of profit maximisation which is regarded as impossible of achievement in a world of uncertainty.

Satisficing theory, as it is commonly known, is closely associated with the work of Simon.[1] He has expressed the essence of his standpoint as follows:[2] 'We must expect the firm's goals to be not maximising profits, but attaining a certain level or rate of profit, holding a certain share of the market or a certain level of sales. Firms would try to "satisfice" rather than to maximize.' In his opinion there is considerable empirical evidence that business goals are stated in satisficing terms. He refers first to the studies which indicate that businessmen often set prices by applying a standard mark-up to costs. (See the section on pricing policy, pp. 91–8.) He also refers to alternative sources such as the study by Cyert and March,[3] who found in one industry some evidence that firms with a declining share of their markets strove more vigorously to increase their sales than firms whose shares of the market were steady or increasing.

The notion of satisficing is, however, of rather older origin, and was most clearly expressed by Gordon [4] when he wrote that

In an important sense, the primary aim of a businessman is to stay in business. Given the fog of uncertainty within which he must operate, the limited number of variables his mind can juggle at one time, and his desire to play safe, it would not be at all surprising if he adopted a set of yardsticks that promised reasonably satisfactory profits in the long run and a maximum of stability in his relations with customers, suppliers and competitors. These conditions suggest that many businessmen are likely, as we have already noted, to substitute the principle of satisfactory profits for that of profit maximization. These considerations also suggest . . . that businessmen may seek to use average total rather than marginal cost as a guide in pricing in order to achieve satisfactory profits.

A number of theories have been developed which incorporate the notion of satisficing, and it is, as we shall discover below, an integral part of what is known as the behavioural theory of the firm. In addition to the groundwork laid by Simon it is worth considering in this context the 'deliberative' theory developed by Margolis.[5]

(ii) *Deliberative Theory*

Margolis starts out with the premise that a firm is faced with considerable uncertainty. As a result, a firm may often deliberately ignore an opportunity which offers the prospect of greater profitability than the opportunity which the firm adopts instead. This is because

The firm has adopted a pattern of behaviour which will protect itself from the unknown while seeking ever growing profits. This does not mean that the theorist should feel free to conceive of the firm as acting randomly or imitatively. Instead of assuming either extreme of a complete absence of rational efforts of maximization or the presence of perfect foresight, it would be preferable to assume realistically that the management hopes to achieve more and more profits; that, operating as they must under conditions of uncertainty, the rules and tools they adopt must be quite different from those appropriate to conditions of perfect foresight. The managers, rather than being omniscient at one extreme or mechanically random at the other extreme, are deliberating leaders of a firm who adopt procedures and rules because of the lack of information necessary to be fully 'rational'.[6]

As compared to traditional theories Margolis's model of the 'deliberative' firm (a term which he prefers to 'satisficing' or 'behavioural') 'imposes far fewer demands on necessary knowledge'. Despite this the theory is structured. The firm is motivated to seek better solutions to problems through the adoption of aspiration levels (see pp. 144–5) which must (*a*) 'be high enough to ensure the long run survival of the firm' and (*b*) 'must be equal to or greater than current normal profits'. The firm treats decisions sequentially, selecting a policy which, on the basis largely of current information (itself the outcome of information gathered as a result of implementing previous policies) rather than upon guesses about the future, satisfies the aspiration level then in existence. The firm is thus inefficient according to the criteria of the traditional models, but this inefficiency is simply the 'cost paid to reduce uncertainty'. Provided that the firm bases decisions upon 'current information supplemented by strategical rules based upon past experience' then rational decisions will be forthcoming.[7]

(iii) *Survival*

Almost all theories of the firm make some reference, whether explicit or implicit, to the desire on the part of management for the survival of their firms. This is hardly surprising since managers cannot be expected to pursue goals other than profit maximisation beyond the point at which their own jobs are put in jeopardy. In some cases, however, survival has been promoted to play the part of the firm's predominant objective. Galbraith for example suggests [8] that 'for any organisation, as for any organism, the goal or objective that has a natural assumption of pre-eminence is the organization's own survival'.

In Rothschild's opinion [9] the desire for secure profits is probably of a similar order to the desire for maximum profits. Security implies risk avoidance whereas high profits will, for the most part, arise out of medium- or high-risk projects. Hence a desire for security is unlikely to be synonymous with long-run profit maximisation. As Rothschild points out, a firm bent upon maximising profits will put money into those projects which offer the greatest returns irrespective of whether such projects are internal or external to the firm, whereas a firm bent upon security will always re-invest the bulk of its profits. Galbraith sees this dichotomy as the logical conclusion of the fact that, whereas with low earnings or losses a firm becomes vulnerable to outside influence and loses its autonomy, above a certain level more earnings add little or nothing to its security.[10]

Fellner has suggested the objective of a 'safety margin' [11] which is the difference between the sales price of a commodity and the average unit cost incurred in its production. The safety margin then allows for unexpected price falls or rises in costs for which the firm cannot compensate itself in the short term, and prevents the subsequent decline in profits from having too severe an impact upon the firm. According to Gordon [12] a businessman operates in such a state of uncertainty that 'he may well take the sort of action which yields a substantial margin of safety and particularly the sort of action which promises to stabilize one or more of the variables with which he has to deal'.

Aigner, Day and Smith [13] investigated the possibility of determining a compromise between expected profit maximisation and high safety margins. They concluded that

> the desire to cover overheads and hence to avoid losses in the presence of uncertainty about price or the position of the monopolist's demand curve results in various output policies which can be most simply characterized as full cost pricing or safety margin pricing. In some cases behaviour satisfies conventional $MC = MR$ rules so long as it does not isolate a bound placed by the desire for safety first. However in general a concern for safety margins will lead to a departure from conventional rules.

(iv) *Internal Finance*

As suggested above the desire for security will tend to lead to re-investment of profits. This effect can alternatively be regarded as a desire to avoid a liquidity crisis. Reder [14] argues that management may have to accept some form of trade-off between liquidity and profitability where a firm seeks to finance its expansion out of retained earnings. Dean [15] points out that many firms prefer relatively liquid investments even at the expense of some loss of profits, and Gordon [16] suggests that 'economists tend to underrate the importance of what may be called the liquidity-solvency motive in business. The fear of bankruptcy and the even more widespread fear of temporary financial embarrassment are probably more powerful drives than the desire for the absolute maximum in profits.' He refers also to the 'banker mentality' which leads in large firms to the sacrifice of probable profits for the sake of an impregnable financial position.[17]

The drawbacks to any theory incorporating the notion of satisficing apply, as we shall discover below, equally to behavioural theory. Lee[18] has summed it up as follows: 'However the vagueness of satisficing as the goal of a firm presents serious problems in building a predictive model of business organizations.' Thus the theories cannot at present be subjected to meaningful statistical testing.

Chapter 21 See also D.C. HAGUE MANAGERIAL ECONS. CHAP 2.

The Behavioural Theory of the Firm

(i) *Introduction*

Dissatisfaction with the traditional theory of the firm has led certain commentators to branch out in a new direction which borrows heavily from the behavioural sciences.

At heart the behavioural theory of the firm attempts to replace the traditional normative approach to the analysis of firms' behaviour with a much more positive approach. Classical economic theory is normative in the sense of postulating how a firm *should behave* if it is to go about maximising its profits. Traditional organisation theory is also normative in so far that it postulates the *ideal structure* for different sorts of organisation. Ideas on the structure of organisations tended to originate from the analysis of existing institutions such as the churches and the armed forces. In such institutions the individual is treated as subordinate to the organisation, and his functions are spelled out for him as part of the over-all scheme of relationships between individuals within the organisation. This allocation of roles is, however, unacceptable to modern behavioural theorists who emphasise the fact that individuals do not fit into neat little slots but rather have needs and goals which do not tally exactly with those of the employing institutions. The behaviourist approach is therefore positive rather than normative, and involves an attempt to find ways of describing how firms actually operate in practice.

Behavioural theorists set out to analyse the process by which firms decide upon their objectives, which are multiple rather than single. However, in any situation where a firm has several objectives the need arises to strike some kind of balance between them, and this implies the existence of conflict. Behavioural theorists are interested to discover how such conflict arises, what form it takes, and how it is resolved. In this context they treat every objective as a constraint upon the firm's behaviour, since the firm must achieve all of its objectives at the same time. However, unlike the traditional models, the solution to the conflict situation is invariably sub-optimal.

The most comprehensive outline of behavioural theory is contained in Cyert and March,[1] and the following section is largely a summary of ideas expressed therein. Once again our starting point is the separation of ownership from control. The firm is run by salaried managers who have certain personal objectives which they pursue in their day-to-day work. Such managers are not, however, solely interested in maximising their personal rewards. They feel a strong affiliation both with the firm for which they work and in particular with their own department within that firm, and they derive substantial personal satisfaction from such affiliations. Nevertheless, the varying personal motivations of individual managers and their desire to promote their own department, even at the expense of other departments within the firm, inevitably creates conflict both between individuals and between departments. Such conflicts must necessarily be resolved if the firm is not to deteriorate into a state of anarchy whereby different departments go their own way without paying much regard to the best interests of the firm as a whole. Some means must therefore be found of running the firm more or less to everyone's satisfaction.

(ii) *Coalitions*

In practice, the conflict situation will encompass more than just the managerial group since that group is not freed from all external constraints upon its behaviour. Cyert and March accordingly introduce the concept of the *coalition* which is defined to include everyone who has reason to expect anything from the firm. The composition of the coalition varies over time, but in general incorporates the firm's managers, shareholders, customers, employees and creditors. Immediately this raises the question as to how such a group of divergent interests can come to agree upon a set of objectives for the firm. Cyert and March suggest that most of the coalition members tend to take no great interest in the specific objectives of the firm provided that they receive a satisfactory stream of *side-payments* from the firm. The existence of side-payments was implicit in the traditional theory of the firm where the entrepreneur, or sole decision-taker, bought off interference from outside interests by paying a sufficiently high level of wages to his employees and of dividends to his shareholders; by producing a product which satisfied his customers; and paying off his creditors in good time. In much the same way the managers of a modern corporation can buy off interference from shareholders, employees and customers, and thus remove a possible source of conflict in the setting of the firm's objectives.

(iii) *Goals*

The passivity of the majority of coalition members does not by itself remove every potential source of conflict, because we are still left with conflict between individual managers and between departments within the firm. The idea of side-payments is again useful, because certain managers can be rewarded with higher salaries or greater prestige in return for their agreement not to participate in the decision-making process. However, most of the management group will expect to have a hand in decision-making, especially when the annual budget plans are up for discussion or when the firm is considering branching out in new directions. Cyert and March consider that the intra-management bargaining over objectives will generate one set of objectives which are *quantitative* and another set which are *qualitative*.

In the latter case we are referring to objectives which have no operational content, and which do not require that specific action be taken if they are to be fulfilled. Such objectives are typified by the slogans, 'Our aim is to please', or, 'Our aim is to produce high-quality products'. It is evident that almost any managerial decision can be justified by reference to such superficially impressive slogans, and qualitative objectives therefore serve to minimise the amount of conflict by inducing all managers to believe that they share at least some communally agreed objectives.

Nevertheless, the firm also needs to have a set of quantifiable objectives which can be translated into specific courses of action. Cyert and March suggest that the following five goals are the most important.

(1) *The Production Goal.* The production department is largely concerned with matters of output and employment. Its members want their machinery to be fully utilised so that the work-force can be retained. They also want the fewest possible number of change-overs from making one product to making another because of the disruptive effects of such change-overs upon the smooth running of their department. Long production runs also make production scheduling much easier, and keep down costs. If sales are poor the production department will want an increase in inventories rather than a cut in output.
(2) *The Inventory Goal.* This implies a desire to avoid running out of stocks, whether of raw materials (which would annoy the production department) or of finished goods (which would annoy both the sales force and the firm's customers). The holding of inventories therefore pleases both sales and production departments, but conflicts with the interests of the financial managers who regard the holding of excessive inventories as unprofitable, since it ties up valuable working capital.
(3) *The Level of Sales Goal.* This can be defined in terms of either revenue or of output, but in either case implies the possibility of conflict should the sales force attempt to increase sales without paying due regard to their profitability.
(4) *The Market-Share Goal.* This reflects an interest in the firm's standing in its various markets relative to its competitors. Conflict may arise from the pursuit of this goal in the same way as for the level of sales goal.
(5) *The Profit Goal.* Profit is obviously necessary for the firm's continued existence because of the on-going need to pay dividends and to fund the firm's future growth. In spite of the considerable difficulties in calculating profit it is often taken as a guide to the firm's performance because no better index of efficiency exists. Furthermore, it is possible to make inter-firm profit comparisons.

To a greater or lesser extent all managers are interested in the profit goal, but in most cases they may be willing to sacrifice profit in order to achieve other goals. Profit maximisation is, in general, incompatible with the simultaneous pursuit of alternative goals. — OBJECTIVE IS SATISFICING - maximisation of no particular goal

(iv) *Aspiration Levels*

Associated with each of the quantitative objectives as outlined above there is an *aspiration level*. An aspiration level signifies a desire on the part of the management group to improve upon, repeat, or fall short of the previous year's performance during the forthcoming year. Given the variability of the environment within which the firm has to operate one might well expect aspiration levels to fluctuate widely over time. Cyert and March, however, expect aspiration levels to fluctuate relatively little. They argue that the stability of aspirations largely arises from the methods by which decisions are taken within corporations. There is an observed tendency for corporations to become bureaucratic and to establish sets of written rules concerning the conduct of substantial areas of the firm's operations. These rules are laid down after lengthy discussions by committees, and, once established, tend to be treated with some reverence, despite the fact that the firm's environment may be undergoing rapid change. These rules are often financial in nature, appearing in the form of budgets and operating standards which greatly constrain the scope of the individual manager for unorthodox behaviour.

The establishment of financial constraints has several advantages. First, it makes it possible for any level of the firm's managerial hierarchy to keep a close eye upon the performance of subordinate managers since there is provision for this to be compared at regular intervals against the previously agreed targets. Secondly, it is a good deal easier for all concerned to adhere to whatever has been established by precedent rather than to be continually questioning the relevance of yesterday's rules to today's environment. Thus there is a tendency to assume that what was agreed upon last time around should not be materially altered with respect to the forthcoming period.

It is therefore to be expected that aspirations will change slowly but steadily rather than rapidly and erratically. This is not to imply, however, that aspirations are necessarily unrealistic. No manager will want to commit himself to targets which are almost certain to be beyond his reach, nor will upper management allow subordinates to commit themselves to targets which present no real challenge. Hence if a firm produces an unusually good or bad performance extra care will be taken to adjust aspirations accordingly. This is of much greater importance where the firm falls well short of meeting one or more of its quantitative goals, and when this happens *search behaviour* will be instigated in order to discover the cause of the failure. Should this turn out to be human in origin the remedy falls easily to hand. Where, however, the failure arises from what appears to be a lasting unfavourable alteration in the firm's environment it becomes necessary for the firm to adjust aspirations by an appreciable amount in a downwards direction in order to keep them in line with the new reality. However, this kind of search operation will only take place when performance falls well short of the target level. There is little likelihood that a firm will search out ways of improving its efficiency so long as targets are, by and large, being met, despite the fact that aspirations may frequently fall well below what could potentially be achieved were the firm to respond to smaller variations in market conditions.

Another drawback to the above methods of adjusting aspirations is that they lead to inconsistencies between objectives. At some point in time a firm will establish a mutually consistent set of objectives, and, provided that the environment remains stable, there is no reason why aspirations cannot be adjusted in such a way as to retain the consistency between objectives. But the onset of a crisis situation in which some targets are being met (for example, for market share and level of sales) but not others (for example, for profits) will tend to result in changed aspirations which are no longer mutually consistent, since a firm is unlikely to alter its aspirations with respect to targets which are being met as much as for targets which are way above what has been achieved in practice.

(v) *Organisational Slack*

In circumstances in which aspiration levels change slowly but in which the firm's environment fluctuates a good deal, one would expect the firm to perform either considerably better or considerably worse than it had anticipated. But if it does much better than expected how does the firm absorb the excess revenues? And from where can the firm obtain unused resources in order to make up the shortfall when performance falls short of target? The answer to both of these questions is to be found in the concept of *organisational slack*. Cyert and March argue that the members of the coalition are often paid in excess of their opportunity costs. Wages, salaries, and profits are generally higher than they need to be in order to keep managers, workers and shareholders happy. Alternatively, creditors may be paid unnecessarily quickly, and prices may be kept below what the market will bear. This is due in part to the difficulties inherent in trying to assess accurately the correct level at which various financial magnitudes should be set, but it may also reflect an indifference on the part of the firm to holding down costs to their lowest possible level.

There are thus several unutilised sources of profits; first, in the surplus payments to coalition members; secondly, where factor inputs of all types are not being utilised either fully or efficiently; and thirdly, where the firm pursues sub-optimal pricing, production, or marketing strategies.

Thus, at times when the firm does much better than expected, it allows slack to develop so as to absorb the difference between aspiration and actual performance. For example, wages and salaries are allowed to rise and unprofitable investments are undertaken. Where, however, the firm subsequently falls upon hard times it can make up the difference between aspiration and actual performance by eliminating previously accumulated slack. For example, managerial perks can be removed, a wage claim rejected, prices raised, or a drive to increase productivity set in motion.

One difficulty is that a firm tends to find itself in an ambivalent situation when slack arises. On the one hand, slack implies that the firm is operating at an unnecessarily high level of costs but, on the other hand, it cannot afford to eliminate the slack for fear of what might happen in less satisfactory trading conditions without slack to act as a cushion on which to fall back.

Turning once again to our five quantitative goals enumerated above, we can apply to them the logic of the preceding discussion. The firm has an aspiration level with respect to each individual goal. Although the goals are inconsistent it is possible to satisfy them all simultaneously provided that the firm is satisficing rather than profit maximising. The holding of excessive inventories does not necessarily conflict with the profit goal, although it will clearly do so at times when the profit goal is not being achieved. In the latter event, search behaviour will be initiated and continued until some source of slack has been identified and eliminated, thus increasing profits into line with aspirations. However, no real attempt is likely to be made to eliminate more slack than is strictly necessary in order to meet the profits target. The firm sub-optimises at all times.

(vi) *Assessment of the Model*

Cohen and Cyert do not regard behavioural theory as a substitute for conventional maximisation models. In their opinion [2]

> The behavioural theory is viewed as supplementing the conventional theory of the firm. The traditional theory is essentially one in which certain broad questions are asked. Specifically, the conventional theory of the firm is designed to explain the way in which the price system functions as a mechanism for allocating resources among markets; relatively little is said about resource allocation within the firm. For the purposes of the classical theory, the profit maximization assumption may be perfectly adequate. It is clear however that as one asks a different set of questions, specifically questions designed to uncover the way in which resources are allocated within the firm, the profit maximization assumption is neither necessary nor sufficient for answering these questions. Therefore the behavioural theory of the firm should be viewed as focusing on a different set of questions concerning the internal decision-making structure of the firm.

It can therefore be argued that behavioural models are more realistic than conventional maximisation models. Unfortunately, it is more accurate to refer to behavioural models rather than to *the* behavioural theory of the firm since no two firms behave in an identical fashion. Furthermore, a behavioural model needs to encompass a very wide range of variables, and this makes it very difficult to handle. There is considerable argument about whether it is necessary to construct such complicated models of firms' behaviour, or whether it would be better to concentrate on constructing much simpler models which predict with equivalent accuracy.[3]

Certainly the behavioural models would be much improved if greater account could be taken of the interrelationship between a firm and its environment.[4] In the absence of this development and others the behavioural theory clearly has a long way still to go. As Baumol and Stewart assert [5]

So far the behavioural theorists have offered us as a substitute in this area a variety of fairly general observations, many of them very illuminating; some extremely interesting learning models; and a number of simulation exercises that have added strong evidence that there are rules of thumb, some of them rather simple-minded, governing at least portions of business behaviour. These pieces of analysis have been illuminating and stimulating, but clearly they represent only a beginning along the path the behaviourists have set for themselves.

Notes and References

Chapter 1

1. Useful surveys of the development of economic thought relating to the theory of the firm are to be found in J. M. Clark, *Competition as a Dynamic Process*; S. Lofthouse, *Rivista Internazionale di Scienze Economiche e Commerciali* (Mar 1973 and June 1973); P. J. McNulty, *Journal of Political Economy* (Aug 1967) and *Quarterly Journal of Economics* (Nov 1968); G. J. Stigler, *Journal of Political Economy* (Feb 1957); and C. J. Hawkins, *Theory of the Firm*, ch. 1.

2. A. Smith, *An Inquiry into the Nature and Causes of the Wealth of Nations* (1776).

3. W. S. Jevons, *The Theory of Political Economy* (1871).

4. J. Bentham, *An Introduction to the Principles of Morals and Legislation* (1780).

5. A. Cournot, *Researches into the Mathematical Principles of the Theory of Wealth*.

6. A. Marshall, *Principles of Economics* (1890).

7. See, for example, Lofthouse, *Rivisita Internazionale di Scienze Economiche e Commerciali* (June 1973) pp. 576–7 and Stigler, *Journal of Political Economy* (Feb 1957).

8. According to his *Principles of Economics*, 8th edn (London: Macmillan 1929) p. 540, he did not consider the concept of perfect competition to have empirical validity.

9. J. M. Clark, *The Distribution of Wealth* (New York, 1899).

10. Stigler, *Journal of Political Economy* (Feb 1957) p. 11.

11. Ably assisted by, for example, A. C. Pigou in *Wealth and Welfare* (1912).

12. P. Sraffa, *Economic Journal* (Dec 1926).

13. J. Robinson, *The Economics of Imperfect Competition*.

14. E. H. Chamberlin, *The Theory of Monopolistic Competition*.

15. See also G. J. Stigler, *Five Lectures on Economic Problems* for a detailed discussion of Robinson's and Chamberlin's books.

Chapter 2

1. It is not necessary either that products are identical or that there are no differences in transport costs between firms. What is necessary is that prices should bear a constant relationship to production costs such that all firms earn the same profit per unit in the long run. In order to simplify matters, however, we generally treat all firms as operating along the same cost curves.

2. See Curwen, *Managerial Economics*, ch. 1, for a discussion of the basic cost and revenue concepts which are incorporated in the theory of the firm.

3. Ibid. p. 13.

4. See ibid. p. 6 for a full explanation of the relationship between average and marginal cost.

5. See ibid. pp. 2–7 for a discussion of basic cost concepts.

6. Ibid. pp. 194–206.

7. Chamberlin, *The Theory of Monopolistic Competition*, 6th edn (1948) pp. 214–15.

8. For a full discussion of the welfare aspects of competition and monopoly see F. M. Scherer, *Industrial Market Structure and Economic Performance*, ch. 2.

Chapter 3

1. J. M. Clark, *American Economic Review* (June 1940). See also the *American Economic Review* (May 1955) and *Competition as a Dynamic Process*.

2. This has been reviewed by S. Sosnick in the *Quarterly Journal of Economics* (Aug 1958).

3. Scherer, *Industrial Market Structure and Economic Performance*, p. 37.

4. Ibid. p. 38.

Chapter 4

1. See R. G. Lipsey, *An Introduction to Positive Economics*, p. 252 for a proof of this relationship using calculus.

2. There are a number of alternative ways of measuring monopoly power, as set out, for example, in B. J. McCormick *et al.*, *Introducing*

Economics, pp. 363–6. Unfortunately they all suffer from severe drawbacks.

3. P. E. Hart, M. A. Utton and G. Walshe, *Mergers and Concentration in British Industry* and G. Walshe, *Recent Trends in Monopoly in Great Britain*.

4. M. A. Utton, *Industrial Concentration*.

5. S. Aaronovitch and M. C. Sawyer, *Lloyds Bank Review* (Oct 1974).

6. See Utton, *Industrial Concentration*, ch. 3.

7. R. W. Evely and I. M. D. Little, *Concentration in British Industry*, p. 38.

8. Walshe, *Recent Trends in Monopoly in Great Britain*, p. 4.

9. Ibid. pp. 4, 110–11.

10. Aaronovitch and Sawyer, *Lloyds Bank Review* (Oct 1974) p. 15.

11. See Utton, *Industrial Concentration*, p. 37 for a definition of this term.

12. Walshe, *Recent Trends in Monopoly in Great Britain*, p. 101.

13. Aaronovitch and Sawyer, *Lloyds Bank Review* (Oct 1974) p. 21.

14. For an analysis of U.K. monopoly policy see Curwen, *Managerial Economics*, ch. 6.

Chapter 5

1. See K. J. Cohen and R. M. Cyert, *Theory of the Firm: Resource Allocation in a Market Economy*, ch. 11 for an extension of the above analysis which allows for a relaxation of these assumptions.

2. See ibid. pp. 213–15 for a fuller discussion of all the possible adjustment processes from short-run to long-run equilibrium.

3. See ibid. p. 215, for a mathematical proof, using calculus, that the long-run marginal-cost curve, *LMC*, intersects the marginal-revenue curve, *mr*, at the same output for which *dd* is tangential to LAC.

4. Chamberlin, *Theory of Monopolistic Competition*, 5th edn, p. 81.

5. Stigler, *Five Lectures on Economic Problems*, p. 15.

6. Cohen and Cyert, *Theory of the Firm*, p. 222.

7. In other words any change in price of one product has a negligible effect upon quantity purchased of other products.

8. Stigler, *Five Lectures on Economic Principles*, the relevant one of which is reprinted in *Readings in Industrial Economics*, ed. C. K. Rowley, vol. I, ch. 8, under the title 'Monopolistic Competition in Retrospect'.

9. Chamberlin, *Theory of Monopolistic Competition*, p. 82.

10. Ibid. p. 83.
11. In *Readings in Industrial Economics*, p. 136.
12. Ibid. p. 136.
13. Ibid. p. 136.
14. Ibid. p. 138.
15. See, for example, R. Triffin, *Monopolistic Competition and General Equilibrium Theory*; R. L. Bishop, *American Economic Review* (1952, 1953 and 1955); E. H. Chamberlin, *American Economic Review* (1953) and W. Fellner and R. Heiser in the same issue; E. H. Chamberlin, 'The Chicago School' in *Towards a More General Theory of Value*; G. C. Archibald, *Review of Economic Studies* (Oct 1961); G. J. Stigler, *Review of Economic Studies* (Feb 1963); M. Friedman, *Review of Economic Studies* (Feb 1963); and G. C. Archibald, *Review of Economic Studies* (Feb 1963).
16. R. F. Harrod, *Economic Essays*.
17. Ibid. p. 152.
18. A demand curve can only be tangential to the *LRAC* at the latter's minimum point where the demand curve is perfectly elastic, that is under conditions of perfect competition.
19. See, for example, H. R. Edwards, *Oxford Economic Papers* (Feb 1955); F. H. Hahn, *Oxford Economic Papers* (Oct 1955); P. Streeten, *Oxford Economic Papers* (Oct 1955); and H. F. Lydall, *Oxford Economic Papers* (Oct 1955).
20. Cohen and Cyert, *Theory of the Firm*, p. 225.
21. For example, he argued that if the model was specified with sufficient rigour for it to be used for predictive purposes it would be indistinguishable from the model of perfect competition.
22. Archibald, *Review of Economic Studies* (Oct 1961).
23. M. Friedman, 'The Methodology of Positive Economics' in *Essays in Positive Economics*. See also the *Review of Economic Studies* (Feb 1963).
24. Cohen and Cyert, *Theory of the Firm*, p. 225.
25. Ibid. p. 226.
26. J. Hadar, *Southern Economic Journal* (July 1969).
27. G. C. Archibald, *Economica* (1964) p. 21.
28. This conclusion was contested by K. C. Brown in *Southern Economic Journal* (July 1972) to which Hadar replied in the same issue.
29. J. Hadar and C. Hillinger, *Review of Economic Studies* (Oct 1969).
30. Hawkins, *Theory of the Firm*, p. 26.
31. Lipsey, *An Introduction to Positive Economics*, p. 269.

Chapter 6

1. For this reason it has been held that to understand oligopoly one needs to understand the rules of war: see, for example, K. W. Rothschild, *Economic Journal* (Sep 1947).

Chapter 7

1. A. Cournot, *Researches into the Mathematical Principles of the Theory of Wealth.*
2. H. von Stackelberg, *The Theory of the Market Economy.*
3. R. L. Hall and C. J. Hitch, *Oxford Economic Papers* (May 1939).
4. P. M. Sweezy, *Journal of Political Economy* (Aug 1939).
5. Both instances are cited in Cohen and Cyert, *Theory of the Firm*, pp. 250–53.
6. G. J. Stigler, *Journal of Political Economy* (Oct 1947).
7. J. Simon, *American Economic Review* (Dec 1969).
8. See W. J. Primeaux Jr and M. R. Bomball, *Journal of Political* Economy (July–Aug 1974) p. 852.
9. Ibid. p. 856.
10. Ibid. p. 858.
11. Ibid. p. 859.
12. Ibid. pp. 859–60.
13. See, for example, W. Hamburger, *American Economic Review* (May 1967) pp. 266–72.
14. As suggested by Cohen and Cyert, *Theory of the Firm*, p. 254.
15. See, for example, A. D. Kaplan, J. B. Dirlam, and R. F. Lanzillotti, *Pricing in Big Business: A Case Approach* and Cohen and Cyert, *Theory of the Firm*, pp. 242–4, and pp. 54–6 in this text.
16. See J. Bain, *Journal of Business* (July 1960) p. 197, and for a less extreme view see P. Maunder, *Business Economist* (autumn 1971) p. 136.
17. See, for example, R. F. Lanzillotti, *Review of Economics and Statistics* (Feb 1957) pp. 62–4.
18. As suggested in D. A. Worcester, *Journal of Political Economy* (Aug 1957) and tested with positive results in G. J. Stigler, *Journal of Law and Economics* (Oct 1965). See also pp. 73–6 in this text.
19. Stigler in *Journal of Political Economy* (Oct 1957) illustrates this point using an example taken from the U.S. newsprint industry.
20. Ibid.
21. J. W. Markham, *American Economic Review* (Dec 1951).
22. Bain, *Journal of Business* (July 1960) pp. 200–203.
23. Kaplan, Dirlam, and Lanzillotti, *Pricing in Big Business*, p. 217.

24. Maunder, *Business Economist* (autumn 1972) pp. 139–40 considers that it is extremely difficult to distinguish clearly between any two categories of price leadership.
25. Markham, *American Economic Review* (Dec 1957).
26. See Lanzillotti, *Review of Economics and Statistics* (Feb 1957), and A. Oxenfeldt, *American Economic Review* (June 1952).
27. See, for example, G. J. Stigler, *Journal of Political Economy* (Feb 1964).
28. The richest source of material on cartels is to be found in the case studies undertaken by the Monopolies Commission. See, for example, A. Hunter (ed.), *Monopoly and Competition*, Pt. Four, and pp. 55–6 in this text.
29. Monopolies Commission, *Parallel Pricing*, Cmnd. 5330.
30. Ibid. para. 10.
31. Ibid. para. 27. To the extent that such variations exist a market which apparently manifests the signs of parallel pricing may, in reality, approximate quite closely to conditions of competition.
32. For further discussion of this topic see Maunder, *Business Economist* (autumn 1972) p. 135.
33. G. and P. Polanyi, *Moorgate and Wall St Review* (spring 1974) p. 42. See also Markham, *American Economic Review* (Dec 1951) p. 899.
34. Monopolies Commission, *Parallel Pricing*, p. 13.
35. Such as Markham and the Polanyis.
36. In *Moorgate and Wall St Review* (spring 1974) p. 46.
37. Monopolies Commission, *Parallel Pricing*, p. 37.
38. Ibid. p. 14.
39. Ibid. p. 15.
40. Ibid. p. 22.
41. Ibid. p. 25.
42. Ibid. p. 25.
43. Ibid. p. 26.
44. Ibid. p. 21.
45. Ibid. p. 29.
46. In *Moorgate and Wall St Review* (spring 1974) p. 52.
47. Monopolies Commission, *Parallel Pricing*, p. 28.
48. In *Moorgate and Wall St Review* (spring 1974) pp. 54–8.

Chapter 8

1. Lipsey, *An Introduction to Positive Economics*.
2. The concept of joint profits has a long history, and is for example an integral part of W. Fellner, *Competition Among the Few*.

3. Lipsey, *An Introduction to Positive Economics*, p. 272.
4. Ibid. pp. 272–3.

Chapter 9

1. The original exposition of this theory is to be found in J. von Neumann and O. Morgenstern, *Theory of Games and Economic Behaviour*.
2. See Curwen, *Managerial Economics*, pp. 56–60 for an explanation of this technique.
3. One of the most sophisticated attempts to apply the principles of game theory is to be found in M. Shubik, *Strategy and Market Structure, Competition, Oligopoly and the Theory of Games*. For interesting developments stemming from the basic game situation see, for example, R. D. Luce and H. Raiffa, *Games and Decisions*; L. B. Lave, *Quarterly Journal of Economics* (Aug 1962); and G. W. Nutter, *Southern Economic Journal* (Apr 1964).
4. See, for example, D. K. Osborne, *American Economic Review* (1971) p. 538.
5. For further analysis of the prisoner's dilemma see, for example, L. B. Lave, *Behavioural Science* (Jan 1965); A. Rapoport and C. Orwant, *Behavioural Science* (Jan 1962); and R. Weil, *Behavioural Science* (May 1966).
6. Lave, *Quarterly Journal of Economics* (Aug 1962).
7. F. T. Dolbear *et al.*, 'Collusion in the Prisoner's Dilemma: Number of Strategies', in *Oligopoly. An Empirical Approach*, ed. R. Sherman.
8. Ibid. p. 31.
9. F. T. Dolbear *et al.*, *Quarterly Journal of Economics* (May 1968).
10. L. Fouraker and S. Siegel, *Bargaining Behaviour* (New York: McGraw-Hill, 1963).
11. Much the same conclusion is drawn by J. W. Friedman, *Yale Economic Essays* (autumn 1963).
12. Dolbear *et al.*, *Quarterly Journal of Economics* (May 1968) p. 254.
13. Ibid. p. 258.
14. J. L. Murphy, *Quarterly Journal of Economics* (May 1966).
15. J. W. Friedman, *Econometrica* (July–Oct 1967).
16. Ibid. p. 397.
17. See J. W. Friedman, *Review of Economic Studies* (Oct 1969) for a discussion and critique of a number of important experiments.

Chapter 10

1. See, for example, J. S. Bain, *American Economic Review* (Mar 1949); J. S. Bain, *Barriers to New Competition*; P. Sylos-Labini, *Oligopoly and Technical Progress*; F. Modigliani, *Journal of Political Economy* (June 1958); D. E. Farrar and C. F. Phillips Jr, *Journal of Political Economy* (Aug 1959); D. K. Osborne, *Journal of Political Economy* (Aug 1964); O. E. Williamson, *Quarterly Journal of Economics* (Feb 1963); H. M. Mann, *Review of Economics and Statistics* (Aug 1966); R. Sherman and T. D. Willett, *Journal of Political Economy* (Aug 1967); J. T. Wenders, *Journal of Political Economy* (Oct 1967); B. P. Pashigian, *Journal of Industrial Economics* (July 1968); D. R. Kamerschen, *Journal of Political Economy* (July–Aug 1968); J. N. Bhagwati, *Oxford Economic Papers* (Nov 1970); M. I. Kamien and N. L. Schwartz, *Econometrica* (May 1971); J. T. Wenders, *Journal of Industrial Economics* (Nov 1971); H. A. Cohen, *Mississippi Valley Journal* (winter 1971–2); R. McGuckin, *Southern Economic Journal* (Jan 1972); M. Kamien and N. Schwartz, *American Economic Review* (Dec 1972); W. G. Shepherd, *American Economic Review*, papers and proceedings (May 1973); D. K. Osborne, *Journal of Industrial Economics* (Sep 1973); D. P. Baron, *American Economic Review* (Sep 1973); and D. Orr, *Review of Economics and Statistics* (Feb 1974).

2. N. Kaldor, *Economica*, no. 2 (1935).

3. Harrod, *Economic Essays*, p. 152.

4. Bain, *Barriers to New Competition*.

5. Sylos-Labini, *Oligopoly and Technical Progress*.

6. Some of the drawbacks to this approach are set out in, for example, Osborne, *Journal of Political Economy* (Aug 1964) p. 397.

7. See Bain, *Barriers to New Competition*, pp. 21–2.

8. The reader can demonstrate this possibility for himself by lowering the firms' average-cost curve downwards in Figure 10.1 until OB is greater than OC.

9. Bear in mind, however, that all future profit flows need to be discounted to their present value (a technique explained fully in Curwen, *Managerial Economics*, ch. 5) when assessing the optimal long-run strategy. As a result limit pricing is only likely to be profitable if short-run profit-maximising behaviour would induce a considerable entry of new firms within a short space of time.

10. Following the example of Modigliani in *Journal of Political Economy* (June 1958) p. 217.

11. D. Needham, *Economic Analysis and Industrial Structure*, p. 104 argues, however, that 'There is no such thing as the most unfavourable policy for entrants, short of driving prices down to zero'

(through established firms substantially *increasing* their production once entry has occurred).

12. Sherman and Willett, *Journal of Political Economy* (Aug 1967).

13. Pashigian, *Journal of Industrial Economics* (July 1968) p. 166.

14. Ibid. p. 167.

15. Ibid. p. 166.

16. Williamson, *Quarterly Journal of Economics* (Feb 1963).

17. Stigler, *The Organization of Industry*, pp. 19–20.

18. Empirical evidence supporting this contention is also to be found in Blackstone, *Quarterly Review of Economics and Business* (winter 1972).

19. G. J. Stigler, *The Theory of Price*.

20. Kamien and Schwartz, *Econometrica* (May 1971).

21. Wenders, *Journal of Industrial Economics* (Nov 1971) p. 18.

22. Osborne, *Journal of Political Economy* (Aug 1964) p. 399.

23. Ibid. p. 400.

24. Bain, *Barriers to New Competition*.

25. Ibid. p. 201.

26. Mann, *Review of Economics and Statistics* (Aug 1966).

27. Ibid. p. 298. This finding closely paralleled that of Bain in *Quarterly Journal of Economics* (Aug 1951) pp. 293–4.

28. Ibid. pp. 299–300.

29. Ibid. p. 300.

30. See, for example, Y. Brozen, *Antitrust Bulletin* (spring 1969); H. M. Mann, *Antitrust Bulletin* (winter 1969); S. A. Rhoades, *Journal of Industrial Economics* (Nov 1970); and H. M. Mann, *Journal of Industrial Economics* (July 1971).

31. R. McGuckin, *Southern Economic Journal* (Jan 1972).

32. Wenders, *Journal of Political Economy* (Oct 1967).

33. Orr, *Review of Economics and Statistics* (Feb 1974).

34. R. Low, *Modern Economic Organization*, p. 207.

Chapter 12

1. See, for example, R. S. Koot and D. A. Walker, *Journal of Industrial Economics* (Apr 1970) and A. A. Walters, *Econometrica* (Jan–Apr 1963). A summary is contained in Hawkins, *Theory of the Firm*, pp. 48–9.

2. P. Wiles, *Price, Cost and Output*.

3. A fourth method, namely the use of questionnaires which rely on data supplied by businessmen has also been employed on occasion. There have also been a few attempts, notably by S. Hymer and P. Pashigian, *Journal of Political Economy* (Dec 1962) to infer the shape

of the *LRAC* from information about the growth rates of different-sized firms, but the evidence derived from these studies is, so far, inconclusive. See Needham, *Economic Analysis and Industrial Structure*, pp. 43–6.

4. J. Johnston, *Statistical Cost Analysis*.

5. The first two criticisms are discussed more fully in C. A. Smith, 'Empirical Evidence on Economies of Scale', in *The Theory of the Firm*, ed. G. C. Archibald. The whole range of criticisms is also to be found in Needham, *Economic Analysis and the Industrial Structure*, pp. 40–1.

6. This technique is discussed more fully by Smith in *The Theory of the Firm*, pp. 34–6. Also see C. F. Pratten, R. Dean and A. Silberston, *The Economies of Large Scale Production in British Industry*, and C. F. Pratten, *Economies of Scale in Manufacturing Industry*.

7. A. Silberston, *Economic Journal*, supplement (Mar 1972).

8. Ibid. p. 386.

9. G. J. Stigler, *Journal of Law and Economics* (Oct 1958).

10. T. Saving, *Quarterly Journal of Economics* (Nov 1961).

11. L. Weiss, *Journal of Political Economy* (June 1964).

12. W. Shepherd, *Southern Economic Journal* (July 1967).

13. Saving, *Quarterly Journal of Economics* (Nov 1961).

14. See, for example, Weiss, *Journal of Political Economy* (June 1964) pp. 260–61; Shepherd, *Southern Economic Journal* (July 1967) pp. 115–16; Needham, *Economic Analysis and Industrial Structure*, pp. 42–3; and Low, *Modern Economic Organization*, pp. 178–9.

15. Needham, *Economic Analysis and Industrial Structure*, p. 42.

Chapter 13

1. See also Curwen, *Managerial Economics*, ch. 4.

2. See, for example, Hall and Hitch, *Oxford Economic Papers* (May 1939); I. F. Pearce, *Economica* (May 1956); Kaplan, Dirlam and Lanzillotti, *Pricing in Big Business*; R. F. Lanzillotti, *American Economic Review* (Dec 1958); R. B. Heflebower in *Business Concentration and Price Policy*; W. W. Haynes, *Pricing Decisions in Small Business*; B. Fog, *Industrial Pricing Policies*; G. J. Stigler and J. K. Kindahl, *The Behaviour of Industrial Prices*; and D. C. Hague, *Pricing in Business*.

3. G. C. Means, 'Industrial Prices and their Relative Inflexibility'.

4. See, for example, Stigler and Kindahl, *The Behaviour of Industrial Prices*; G. C. Means, *American Economic Review* (June 1972); and G. J. Stigler and J. K. Kindahl, *American Economic Review* (Sep 1973).

5. Kaplan, Dirlam and Lanzillotti, *Pricing in Big Business*.

6. Cost-plus pricing is closely associated with our previous discus-

sion of entry-forestalling behaviour. G. C. Means, *Pricing, Power and the Public Interest*, p. 236 has suggested, for example, that target pricing can be used whereby 'the price-maker starts with an estimate of the highest rate of profits which will not induce new entrants, and then works back to determine the prices which will just yield this rate of profit when operating at a reasonable proportion of capacity'. See also pp. 76–7 in this text.

7. See, for example, F. Machlup, *The Economics of Sellers Competition*, and Scherer, *Industrial Market Structure and Economic Performance*, pp. 174–8.

8. Hall and Hitch, *Oxford Economic Papers* (May 1939).

9. Ibid. p. 18.

10. Pearce, *Economica* (May 1956).

11. J. S. Earley, *American Economic Review* (Mar 1956).

12. D. C. Hague, *Review of Economic Studies*, vol. XVI p. 144.

13. Kaplan, Dirlam and Lanzillotti, *Pricing in Big Business*, p. 130.

14. Ibid. p. 284.

15. W. L. Baldwin, *Quarterly Journal of Economics* (May 1964) p. 247.

16. Lanzillotti, *American Economic Review* (Dec 1958).

17. For a fuller summary of the Brookings study see Curwen, *Managerial Economics*, pp. 135–40.

18. Haynes, *Pricing Decisions in Small Business.*

19. Fog, *Industrial Pricing Policies.*

20. Cyert and March, *A Behavioural Theory of the Firm*, pp. 146–7.

21. R. C. Skinner, *Journal of Industrial Economics* (July 1970).

22. Ibid. p. 202.

23. J. Sizer, *Journal of Industrial Economics* (Nov 1971) p. 88.

24. Silberston, *Economic Journal* (Sep 1970).

Chapter 14

1. J. Margolis, *Journal of Business* (July 1958) p. 189.

2. See Curwen, *Managerial Economics*, ch. 1.

3. R. A. Gordon, *American Economic Review* (June 1948) p. 287.

4. See, for example, P. J. Drhymes, *International Economic Review* (Sep 1964); S. H. Hyams, *International Economic Review* (Sep 1966); E. Zabel, *International Economic Review* (June 1967); B. P. Stigum, *International Economic Review* (Oct 1969); E. Zabel, *International Economic Review* (Oct 1969); B. P. Stigum, *Quarterly Journal of Economics* (Nov 1969); A. Sandmo, *American Economic Review* (Mar 1971); J. Lintner, 'Optimum or Maximum Corporate Growth Under Uncertainty', in *The Corporate Economy*, ed. R. Marris and A. Wood;

R. N. Batra and A. Ullah, *Journal of Political Economy* (May–June 1974), and especially E. S. Phelps (ed.), *Microeconomic Foundations of Employment and Inflation Theory.*

5. E. S. Phelps and S. G. Winter Jr, 'Optimal Price Policy Under Atomistic Competition', in *Microeconomic Foundations of Employment and Inflation Theory.*

6. Ibid. p. 336.

Chapter 15

1. See, for example, C. Wright Mills, *The Power Elite* (Oxford U.P., 1957).

2. See, for example, V. Perlo, *The Empire of High Finance*; J. M. Chevalier, *Antitrust Bulletin* (spring 1969) feels that the era of control by financial intermediaries is fairly inevitable within the next decade.

3. A. A. Berle and G. C. Means, *The Modern Corporation and Private Property.*

4. J. K. Galbraith, *The New Industrial State*, p. 91.

5. R. J. Larner, *American Economic Review* (Sep 1966).

6. R. J. Larner, *Management Control and the Large Corporation.*

7. Ibid. p. 17.

8. R. Sheehan, *Fortune* (15 June 1967).

9. D. Villarejo, *New University Thought* (autumn 1961 and Feb 1962).

10. His conclusions are, however, criticised by Larner in *Management Control and the Large Corporation*, p. 22.

11. Chevalier, *Antitrust Bulletin* (spring 1969), using the same definition of control, put the figure for owner control at 60 per cent for 1965–6. In his opinion 'the theory of management control rests on insufficient information; it is doubtful that the theory corresponds to reality'.

12. Villarejo, *New University Thought* (Feb 1962) p. 62.

13. C. Beed, *Journal of Economic Studies*, vol. 1, no. 2 (1966).

14. Berle and Means, *The Modern Corporation and Private Property*, p. 84.

15. Beed, *Journal of Economic Studies* (1966) p. 31.

16. See, for example, Perlo, *The Empire of High Finance.*

17. For evidence which supports these assertions with respect to top U.K. companies between 1960 and 1969 see K. Midgley, *Lloyds Bank Review* (Oct 1974) p. 26.

18. This viewpoint was originally postulated by Berle and Means in *The Modern Corporation and Private Property*, and is currently supported by, for example, B. Hindley in the *Journal of Law and Econo-*

mics (Apr 1970) p. 186. Opinion is, however, by no means unanimous as indicated by, for example, L. R. Desfosses and P. Smith in the *Mississippi Valley Journal* (June 1972) pp. 57–69.

19. See, for example, Villarejo, *New University Thought* (autumn 1961) p. 52 for details of directors' shareholdings in the United States.

20. J. R. Wildsmith, *Managerial Theories of the Firm*, p. 8.

21. Ibid. p. 8.

22. Larner, *Management Control and the Large Corporation*, p. 65.

23. Ibid. p. 3.

24. See Midgley, *Lloyds Bank Review* (Oct 1974) for corroborative evidence with respect to the U.K. between 1960 and 1969.

25. G. Tullock, in *Roads to Freedom*, ed. E. Streissler p. 302.

26. B. Hindley, *Economica* (Nov 1969) pp. 428–9.

27. H. Manne, *Journal of Political Economy* (Apr 1965).

28. R. L. Marris, *The Economic Theory of 'Managerial Capitalism'*.

29. See, for example, A. Singh, *Take-Overs* and H. B. Rose and G. D. Newbould, *Moorgate and Wall St Review* (autumn 1967).

30. A. A. Berle, *The 20th Century Capitalist Revolution*.

31. P. C. Dooley, *American Economic Review* (June 1965).

32. Chevalier, *Antitrust Bulletin* (spring 1969).

33. Beed, *Journal of Economic Studies* (1966) pp. 39–40.

34. Hindley, *Economica* (Nov 1969) pp. 430–4 and *Journal of Law and Economics* (Apr 1970) p. 186.

35. Wildsmith, *Managerial Theories of the Firm*, p. 15.

36. However, A. A. Berle argues in the *Quarterly Journal of Economics* (Feb 1965) that 'rare indeed is the corporate administration who decides a corporate problem differently because he has ownership of, or option to buy, a block of his company's shares'.

37. P. Baran and P. Sweezy, *Monopoly Capital*, p. 46.

38. Villarejo, *New University Thought* (autumn 1961) p. 45.

39. Larner, *Management Control and the Large Corporation*, p. 3

40. Beed, *Journal of Economic Studies* (1966) pp. 39–40.

41. Villarejo, *New University Thought* (autumn 1961) p. 60.

42. Sheehan, *Fortune* (15 June 1967) p. 183.

43. Larner, *Management Control and the Large Corporation*, p. 66.

44. L. De Alessi, 'Private Property and Dispersion of Ownership in Large Corporations', *Journal of Finance* (Sep 1973).

45. Ibid. pp. 841, 849.

Chapter 16

1. Baumol, *Economica* (Aug 1958) and *Business Behaviour, Value and Growth*.

2. W. G. Shepherd, *Economica* (Nov 1962).

3. B. D. Mabry and D. Siders, *Southern Economic Journal* (Jan 1967).

4. B. D. Mabry, *Western Economic Journal* (Mar 1968).

5. C. J. Hawkins, *Journal of Industrial Economics* (Apr 1970) pp. 135, 138.

6. C. J. Hawkins, *American Economic Review* (June 1970). But see also T. A. Murphy and Y-K. Ng, *Journal of Industrial Economics* (Mar 1974).

7. A. A. Alchian, *Journal of Industrial Economics* (Nov 1965).

8. Baumol, *Business Behaviour, Value and Growth*, p. 46.

9. A. Patton, *Men, Money, and Motivation.*

10. D. R. Roberts, *Executive Compensation.*

11. J. S. Chiu, A. O. Elbing and J. W. McGuire, *American Economic Review* (Sep 1962).

12. M. Hall, *Journal of Industrial Economics* (Apr 1967).

13. The results of the Hall study are, however, disputed in L. Waverman, *Journal of Industrial Economics* (Nov 1968).

14. Mabry, *Western Economic Journal* (Mar 1968).

15. R. T. Masson, *Journal of Political Economy* (Dec 1971).

16. A point which has its origin in F. W. Taussig and W. S. Barker, *Quarterly Journal of Economics* (Nov 1925).

17. W. G. Llewellen, *Journal of Finance* (May 1969).

18. Larner, *Management Control and the Large Corporation*, p. 61.

Chapter 17

1. W. J. Baumol, *American Economic Review* (Dec 1962).

2. J. H. Williamson, *Economica* (Feb 1966).

3. See, for example, R. Marris, *Quarterly Journal of Economics* (May 1963); *The Economic Theory of 'Managerial Capitalism'*; *Economic Journal*, special issue (Mar 1972); and 'The Modern Corporation and Economic Theory', in *The Corporate Economy*, ed. Marris and Wood, ch. 9.

4. Marris, *Quarterly Journal of Economics* (May 1963) p. 186.

5. Ibid. pp. 187–8.

6. Ibid. pp. 206–7.

7. See Marris, *The Economic Theory of 'Managerial Capitalism'*, ch. 7, and H. A. Simon and C. Bonini, *American Economic Review* (Sep 1958).

8. R. M. Solow, *Public Interest* (spring 1968).

9. D. C. Mueller, *Journal of Industrial Economics* (July 1972).

10. Ibid. pp. 210–16.

11. See also M. Hall and L. Weiss, *Review of Economics and Statistics* (Aug 1967) for some supportive evidence.

12. See, for example, Hawkins, *Theory of the Firm*, pp. 79–80.

13. H. K. Radice, *Economic Journal* (Sep 1971).

14. Ibid. pp. 206–7.

15. R. J. Monsen, J. S. Chiu and D. E. Cooley, *Quarterly Journal of Economics* (Aug 1968) p. 442.

16. D. R. Kamerschen, *Quarterly Journal of Economics* (Nov 1970).

17. Larner, *American Economic Review* (Sep 1966).

18. Hindley, *Journal of Law and Economics* (Apr 1970).

19. Llewellen, *Journal of Finance* (May 1969).

Chapter 18

1. For further details of both homeostasis and viability see L. S. Burns, *University of Washington Business Review* (Oct 1959). See also A. G. Papandreou, in *Survey of Contemporary Economics*, ed. B. Haley, p. 212 for a discussion of the hypothesis of 'selection of the fittest'.

2. See W. B. Cannon, *The Wisdom of the Body*, p. 317.

3. K. E. Boulding, A *Reconstruction of Economics*, pp. 26–7.

4. A. A. Alchian, *Journal of Political Economy* (1950) pp. 211–21.

5. G. Tintner, *Econometrica* (1941).

6. Alchian, *Journal of Political Economy* (1950) p. 215.

7. E. T. Penrose, *American Economic Review* (Dec 1952). See also *American Economic Review* (Sep 1953) pp. 600–7.

Chapter 19

1. J. R. Hicks, *Econometrica* (Jan 1935).

2. T. Scitovsky, *Review of Economic Studies* (1943).

3. J. P. Nettl, *Review of Economic Studies* (Feb 1957).

4. M. W. Reder, *Journal of Political Economy* (1947).

5. Nettl, *Review of Economic Studies* (Feb 1957) is of the opinion that the salaried manager will work harder.

6. Papandreou, in A *Survey of Contemporary Economics*. See also M. Silver, *Journal of Industrial Economics* (Apr 1967) p. 159.

7. Papandreou, in A *Survey of Contemporary Economics*, p. 204.

8. Ibid. p. 213.

9. R. J. Monsen and A. Downs, *Journal of Political Economy* (June 1965) p. 225.

10. Ibid. p. 226.

11. See, for example, O. E. Williamson, 'A Model of Rational Managerial Behaviour', in *A Behavioural Theory of the Firm*, ed. R. M. Cyert and J. G. March; *The Economics of Discretionary Behaviour* and *Corporate Control and Business Behaviour*.

12. Williamson, *The Economics of Discretionary Behaviour*, p. 1034.

13. Ibid. chs. 6, 7.

14. Ibid.

15. H. Leibenstein, *American Economic Review* (June 1966). The ideas contained in his paper were subsequently amended and expanded in the *Quarterly Journal of Economics* (Nov 1969 and May 1972); and the *Journal of Political Economy* (May–June 1973).

16. Ibid. p. 413.

17. As set out, for example, in M. A. Crew, M. Jones-Lee and C. K. Rowley, *Southern Economic Journal* (Oct 1971). See also the papers by Leibenstein previously cited; W. S. Comanor and H. Leibenstein, *Economica* (Aug 1969); M. A. Crew and C. K. Rowley, *Economica* (May 1971); M. A. Crew and C. K. Rowley, *Economic Journal* (Dec 1972); Y-K. Ng and R. Parish, *Economica* (Aug 1972); J. P. Shelton, *American Economic Review* (Dec 1967); and C. K. Rowley, *Antitrust and Economic Efficiency*.

18. This has led M. Howe to suggest in 'Anti-trust policy, Rules or Discretionary Intervention?', *Moorgate and Wall St Review* (Feb 1971) that X-inefficiency may not increase in line with monopoly power since a large firm may well be able to offer better incentives than its smaller brethren.

19. This point is discussed in Rowley, *Antitrust and Economic Efficiency*, pp. 27–8; and K. J. Blois, *Quarterly Journal of Economics* (May 1972).

20. See, for example, Marris, *The Economic Theory of 'Managerial Capitalism'*; Williamson, *The Economics of Discretionary Behaviour*; and Cyert and March, *A Behavioural Theory of the Firm*.

21. C. K. Rowley, *Steel and Public Policy*.

22. Leibenstein, *Quarterly Journal of Economics* (Nov 1969) pp. 612–20.

23. See, for example, E. Mansfield, *The Economics of Technological Change*, pp. 100–3.

Chapter 20

1. See, for example, H. A. Simon, *Quarterly Journal of Economics* (Feb 1955); *American Economic Review* (June 1959); and *American Economic Review*, papers and proceedings (May 1962).

2. Simon, *American Economic Review* (June 1959).
3. R. M. Cyert and J. G. March, 'Organisational Factors in the Theory of the Firm', *Quarterly Journal of Economics* (Feb 1956).
4. Gordon, *American Economic Review* (June 1948) pp. 270–1.
5. Margolis, *Journal of Business* (July 1958).
6. Ibid. p. 189.
7. D. Bodenhorn, *Journal of Business* (Apr 1959) p. 172 argues that Margolis's theory will lead to essentially the same predictions as traditional theory. Margolis disagrees in an article in the same issue.
8. Galbraith, *The New Industrial State*, p. 175. See also P. Drucker, *Journal of Business* (Apr 1958) for a theory which revolves around the question of survival. The desire for security is a major theme running through Marris, *The Economic Theory of 'Managerial Capitalism'* and recurs in E. S. Mason (ed.), *The Corporation in Modern Society*.
9. K. W. Rothschild, *Economic Journal* (Sep 1947) pp. 308–9.
10. Galbraith, *The New Industrial State*, p. 176.
11. W. Fellner, *Competition Among the Few*, pp. 153–4.
12. Gordon, *American Economic Review* (June 1948) p. 270.
13. D. J. Aigner, R. H. Day and K. R. Smith, *Journal of Political Economy* (Dec 1971).
14. Reder, *Journal of Political Economy* (1947).
15. J. Dean, *Managerial Economics*.
16. Gordon, *American Economic Review* (June 1948) p. 271.
17. See also Boulding, *American Economic Review* (May 1952) p. 40, and W. W. Cooper, *Quarterly Journal of Economics* (Feb 1951).
18. C. A. Lee, 'Organization Theory and Business Behaviour', in *Interdisciplinary Studies in Business Behaviour*, ed. J. W. McGuire, p. 62.

Chapter 21

1. Cyert and March, *A Behavioural Theory of the Firm*.
2. Cohen and Cyert, *Theory of the Firm*, p. 330.
3. See, for example, the discussion in Hawkins, *Theory of the Firm*, pp. 72–3.
4. As suggested by Lee in *Studies in Business Behaviour*, pp. 65–6, and W. J. Baumol and M. Stewart, 'On the Behavioural Theory of the Firm', in *The Corporate Economy*, ed. R. Marris and A. Wood, p. 137.
5. Ibid. p. 140.

Bibliography

S. AARONOVITCH and M. C. SAWYER, 'The Concentration of British Manufacturing', *Lloyds Bank Review* (Oct 1974).

D. J. AIGNER, R. H. DAY and K. R. SMITH, 'Safety Margins and Profit Maximization in the Theory of the Firm', *Journal of Political Economy* (Dec 1971).

A. A. ALCHIAN, 'Uncertainty, Evolution, and Economic Theory', *Journal of Political Economy* (1959) pp. 211–21.

—, 'The Basis of Some Recent Advances in the Theory of Management of the Firm', *Journal of Industrial Economics* (Nov 1965).

K. A. ANDREWS, 'Public Responsibility in the Private Corporation', *Journal of Industrial Economics* (Apr 1972).

P. W. ANDREWS, *On Competition in Economic Theory* (London: Macmillan, 1964).

R. N. ANTHONY, 'The Trouble with Profit Maximization', *Harvard Business Review* (1960).

G. C. ARCHIBALD, 'Chamberlin *versus* Chicago', *Review of Economic Studies* (Oct 1961).

—, 'Reply to Chicago', *Review of Economic Studies* (Feb 1963).

—, 'Profit Maximizing and Non-Price Competition', *Economica* (1964) pp. 13–22.

— (ed.), *The Theory of the Firm* (Harmondsworth: Penguin, 1971).

J. S. BAIN, *Barriers to New Competition* (Harvard U.P., 1956).

—, 'Price Leaders, Barometers, and Kinks', *Journal of Business* (July 1960).

—, 'A Note on Pricing in Monopoly and Oligopoly', *American Economic Review* (Mar 1949).

—, 'Relation of Profit Rate to Industry Concentration 1936–40', *Quarterly Journal of Economics* (Aug 1951).

W. L. BALDWIN, 'The Motives of Managers, Environmental Restraints, and the Theory of Managerial Enterprise', *Quarterly Journal of Economics* (May 1964).

P. BARAN and P. SWEEZY, *Monopoly Capital* (Harmondsworth: Penguin, 1968).

D. P. BARON, 'Limit Pricing and Models of Potential Entry', *Western Economic Journal* (Sep 1972).

—, 'Limit pricing, Potential Entry, and Barriers to Entry', *American Economic Review* (Sep 1973).

R. N. BATRA and A. ULLAH, 'Competitive Firm and the Theory of Input Demand Under Price Uncertainty', *Journal of Political Economy* (May–June 1974).

W. J. BAUMOL, 'On the Theory of Oligopoly', *Economica* (Aug 1958).

—, *Business Behaviour, Value and Growth* (New York: Macmillan, 1959).

—, 'On the Theory of Expansion of the Firm', *American Economic Review* (Dec 1962).

—, *Economic Theory and Operations Analysis* (Englewood Cliffs, N.J.: Prentice-Hall, 1965).

W. J. BAUMOL, P. HEIM, B. G. MALKIEL and R. E. QUANDT, 'Earnings Retention, New Capital and the Growth of the Firm', *Review of Economics and Statistics* (Nov 1970).

W. J. BAUMOL and M. STEWART, 'On the Behavioural Theory of the Firm', in *The Corporate Economy*, ed. R. Marris and A. Wood (London: Macmillan, 1971) ch. 5.

C. BEED, 'The Separation of Ownership from Control', *Journal of Economic Studies*, University of Aberdeen, vol. 1, no. 2 (1966).

A. A. BERLE, *The 20th Century Capitalist Revolution* (New York: Harcourt, Brace & Co., 1954).

—, 'The Impact of the Corporation on Classical Economic Theory', *Quarterly Journal of Economics* (Feb 1965).

A. A. BERLE and G. C. MEANS, *The Modern Corporation and Private Property*, revised edition (New York: Harcourt, Brace & World, 1968).

J. BHAGWATI, 'Oligopoly Theory, Entry Prevention, and Growth', *Oxford Economic Papers* (Nov 1970).

R. L. BISHOP, 'Elasticities, Cross Elasticities and Market Relationships', *American Economic Review* (1952).

—, 'Monopolistic Competition After Thirty Years: The Impact on General Theory', *American Economic Review*, papers and proceedings (May 1964).

K. BLOIS, 'A Note on X-Efficiency and Profit Maximization', *Quarterly Journal of Economics* (May 1972).

D. BODENHORN, 'A Note on the Theory of the Firm', *Journal of Business* (Apr 1959).

K. E. BOULDING, 'Implications for General Economics of More Realistic Theories of the Firm', *American Economic Review* (May 1952).

—, *A Reconstruction of Economics* (New York: Wiley, 1950).

M. BRONFENBRENNER, 'Imperfect Competition on a Long-Run Basis', *Journal of Business* (Apr 1950).

K. C. BROWN, 'On the Predictive Content of Models of Monopolistic Competition: Comment', *Southern Economic Journal* (July 1972).

—, 'On the Predictive Content of Models of Monopolistic Competition: Reply', *Southern Economic Journal* (July 1972).

Y. BROZEN, 'Barriers Facilitate Entry', *Antitrust Bulletin* (winter 1969).

—, 'Significance of Profit Data for Anti-trust Policy', *Antitrust Bulletin* (spring 1969).

G. BURCK, 'The Myths and Realities of Corporate Pricing', *Fortune* Apr 1972).

L. S. BURNS, 'Recent Theories of the Behaviour of Business Firms', *University of Washington Business Review* (Oct 1959).

A. CAIRNCROSS, 'The Optimum Firm Reconsidered', *Economic Journal* (Mar 1972).

W. B. CANNON, *The Wisdom of the Body* (New York: Norton, 1932).

E. H. CHAMBERLIN, *The Theory of Monopolistic Competition*, 5th edn (Harvard U.P., 1933).

—, 'Elasticities, Cross-Elasticities and Market Relationships: Comment', *American Economic Review* (1953).

—, *Towards a More General Theory of Value* (New York: Oxford U.P., 1957).

J. M. CHEVALIER, 'The Problem of Control in Large American Corporations', *Antitrust Bulletin* (spring 1969).

J. S. CHIU, A. O. ELBING and J. W. MCGUIRE, 'Executive Incomes, Sales, and Profits', *American Economic Review* (Sep 1962).

J. M. CLARK, 'Toward a Concept of Workable Competition', *American Economic Review* (June 1940).

—, 'Competition. Static Models and Dynamic Aspects', *American Economic Review* (May 1955).

—, *Competition as a Dynamic Process* (Washington D.C.: The Brookings Institution, 1961).

H. A. COHEN, 'Effects of Demand and Cost Changes on the "Limit Price" ', *Mississippi Valley Journal* (winter 1971–2).

K. J. COHEN and R. M. CYERT, *Theory of the Firm: Resource Allocation in a Market Economy* (Englewood Cliffs, N.J.: Prentice-Hall, 1965).

K. J. COHEN and R. M. CYERT, 'Strategy: Formulation, Implementation and Monitoring', *Journal of Business* (July 1973).

W. S. COMANOR and H. LEIBENSTEIN, 'Allocative Efficiency, X-Efficiency and the Measurement of Welfare Loss', *Economica* (Aug 1969).

W. W. COOPER, 'Theory of the Firm – Some Suggestions for Revision', *American Economic Review* (1949).

—, 'A Proposal for Extending the Theory of the Firm', *Quarterly Journal of Economics* (Feb 1951).

A. COURNOT, *Researches into the Mathematical Principles of the Theory of Wealth* (London: Macmillan, 1897).

M. A. CREW, M. JONES-LEE and C. K. ROWLEY, 'X-Theory versus Management Discretion Theory', *Southern Economic Journal* (Oct 1971).

—, and C. K. ROWLEY, 'On Allocative Efficiency, X-Efficiency and the Measurement of Welfare Loss', *Economica* (May 1971).

—, and C. K. ROWLEY, 'A Note on X-Efficiency', *Economic Journal* (Dec 1972).

P. J. CURWEN, *Managerial Economics* (London: Macmillan, 1974).

R. M. CYERT and K. D. GEORGE, 'Competition, Growth and Efficiency', *Economic Journal* (Mar 1969).

R. M. CYERT and C. L. HEDRICK, 'Theory of the Firm: Past, Present and Future. An Interpretation', *Journal of Economic Literature* (June 1972).

R. M. CYERT and M. I. KAMIEN, 'Behavioural Rules and the Theory of the Firm', in *Prices: Issues in Theory, Practice and Public Policy*, ed. A. Phillips and O. E. Williamson (Philadelphia: Pennsylvania U.P., 1967).

R. M. CYERT and J. G. MARCH, 'Organisation, Structure, and Pricing Behaviour in an Oligopolistic Market', *American Economic Review* (Mar 1955).

—, *A Behavioural Theory of the Firm* (Englewood Cliffs, N.J.: Prentice-Hall, 1963).

J. DAVIES, 'On the Sales Maximization Hypothesis. A Comment', *Journal of Industrial Economics* (Apr 1973).

J. DEAN, *Managerial Economics* (Englewood Cliffs, N.J.: Prentice-Hall, 1951).

H. DEMSETZ, 'The Nature of Equilibrium in Monopolistic Competition', *Journal of Political Economy* (Feb 1959).

L. R. DESFOSSES and P. SMITH, 'Interlocking Directorates. A Study of Influence', *Mississippi Valley Journal* (June 1972).

S. T. DOLBEAR, L. B. LAVE, G. BOWMAN, A. LIEBERMAN, E. PRESCOTT,

F. REUTER and R. SHERMAN, 'Collusion in Oligopoly; An Experiment on the Effect of Numbers and Information', *Quarterly Journal of Economics* (May 1968).

P. C. DOOLEY, 'The Interlocking Directorate', *American Economic Review* (June 1969).

P. J. DRHYMES, 'On the Theory of the Monopolistic Multiproduct Firm Under Uncertainty', *International Economic Review* (Sep 1964).

P. DRUCKER, 'Business Objectives and Survival Needs', *Journal of Business* (Apr 1958).

J. S. EARLEY, 'Recent Development in Cost Accounting and the "Marginal Analysis" ', *Journal of Political Economy* (1955) pp. 227–42.

—, 'Marginal Policies of "Excellently Managed" Companies', *American Economic Review* (Mar 1956).

H. R. EDWARDS, 'Price Formation in Manufacturing Industry and Excess Capacity', *Oxford Economic Papers* (Feb 1955).

A. EICHNER, 'A Theory of the Determination of the Mark-Up Under Oligopoly', *Economic Journal* (Dec 1973).

R. W. EVELY and I. M. D. LITTLE, *Concentration in British Industry* (Cambridge U.P., 1960).

D. E. FARRAR and C. E. PHILLIPS Jr, 'New Developments on the Oligopoly Front: A Comment', *Journal of Political Economy* (Aug 1959).

W. FELLNER, *Competition Among the Few* (New York: Knopf, 1949).

—, 'Elasticities, Cross-Elasticities and Market Relationships: Comment', *American Economic Review* (1953).

F. M. FISHER, 'New Developments on the Oligopoly Front: Cournot and the Bain–Sylos Analysis', *Journal of Political Economy* (Aug 1959).

B. FOG, *Industrial Pricing Policies* (Amsterdam: North-Holland, 1960).

J. W. FRIEDMAN, 'Individual Behaviour in Oligopolistic Markets', *Yale Economic Essays* (autumn 1963).

—, 'An Experimental Study of Co-operative Duopoly', *Econometrica* (July–Oct 1967).

—, 'On Experimental Research in Oligopoly', *Review of Economic Studies* (Oct 1969).

M. FRIEDMAN, *Essays in Positive Economics* (Chicago U.P., 1953).

—, 'More on Archibald *versus* Chicago', *Review of Economic Studies* (Feb 1963).

A. GABOR and I. PEARCE, 'A New Approach to the Theory of the Firm', *Oxford Economic Papers* (Oct 1952).

J. K. GALBRAITH, *The New Industrial State* (Harmondsworth: Penguin, 1974).

D. W. GASKINS Jr, 'Dynamic Limit Pricing: Optimal Pricing Under Threat of Entry', *Journal of Economic Theory* (Sep 1971).

W. A. H. GODLEY and C. GILLION, 'Pricing Behaviour in Manufacturing Industry', *National Institute of Economic and Social Research Review* (Aug 1965).

R. A. GORDON, *Business Leadership in the Large Corporation* (University of Carolina Press, 1945).

—, 'Short Period Price Determination in Theory and Practice', *American Economic Review* (June 1948).

J. HADAR, 'On the Predictive Content of Models of Monopolistic Competition', *Southern Economic Journal* (July 1969).

J. HADAR and C. HILLINGER, 'Imperfect Competition with Unknown Demand', *Review of Economic Studies* (Oct 1969).

D. C. HAGUE, 'Economic Theory and Business Behaviour', *Review of Economic Studies*, vol. XVI, pp. 144–59.

—, *Pricing in Business* (London: Allen & Unwin, 1971).

F. H. HAHN, 'Excess Capacity and Imperfect Competition', *Oxford Economic Papers* (1955) pp. 230–40.

M. HALL, 'Sales Revenue Maximization. An Empirical Examination', *Journal of Industrial Economics* (Apr 1967).

M. HALL and L. WEISS, 'Firm Size and Profitability', *Review of Economics and Statistics* (Aug 1967).

R. L. HALL and G. J. HITCH, 'Price Theory and Business Behaviour', *Oxford Economic Papers* (May 1939).

W. HAMBURGER, 'Conscious Parallelism and the Kinked Oligopoly Demand Curve', *American Economic Review*, Papers and Proceedings (May 1967).

R. F. HARROD, *Economic Essays* (New York: Harcourt, Brace & Co., 1952).

P. E. HART, M. A. UTTON and G. WALSHE, *Mergers and Concentration in British Industry* (Cambridge U.P., 1973).

C. J. HAWKINS, 'On the Sales Revenue Maximization Hypothesis', *Journal of Industrial Economics* (Apr 1970).

—, 'The Revenue Maximization Oligopoly Model. Comment', *American Economic Review* (June 1970).

—, *Theory of the Firm* (London: Macmillan, 1973).

C. J. HAWKINS and D. W. PEARCE, *Capital Investment Appraisal* (London: Macmillan, 1971).

W. W. HAYNES, *Pricing Decisions in Small Business* (Lexington: Kentucky U.P., 1962).

R. B. HEFLEBOWER, 'Full Costs, Cost Changes and Prices', in *Business Concentration and Price Policy*, National Bureau of Economic Research (Princeton U.P., 1955).

—, 'Stability in Oligopoly', *Manchester School* (Jan 1961).
K. HEIDENSOHN and N. ROBINSON, *Business Behaviour* (Oxford: Philip Allan, 1974).
J. F. HELLIWELL and C. T. MAO, 'Investment Decision Under Uncertainty, Theory and Practice', *Journal of Finance* (May 1969).
J. R. HICKS, 'Annual Survey of Economic Theory: The Theory of Monopoly', *Econometrica* (Jan 1935).
B. HIGGINS, 'Elements of Indeterminancy in the Theory of Non-Perfect Competition', *American Economic Review* (Sep 1939).
B. HINDLEY, 'Capitalism and the Corporation', *Economica* (Nov 1969).
—, 'Separation of Ownership and Control in the Modern Corporation', *Journal of Law and Economics* (Apr 1970).
E. E. HOOGSTRAAT, 'Attacks on the Value of the Profit Motive in Theories of Business Behaviour', in *Interdisciplinary Studies in Business Behaviour*, ed. J. W. McGuire (Cincinatti: South-Western, 1962).
I. HOROWITZ, *Decision Making and the Theory of the Firm* (New York: Holt, Rinehart & Winston, 1970).
A. HUNTER (ed.), *Monopoly and Competition* (Harmondsworth: Penguin, 1971).
B. HUNTSMAN and W. LLEWELLEN, 'Managerial Pay and Corporate Performance', *American Economic Review* (Sep 1970).
S. H. HYAMS, 'The Price-Taker: Uncertainty, Utility and the Supply Function', *International Economic Review* (Sep 1966).
S. HYMER and P. PASHIGIAN, 'Firm Size and Rate of Growth', *Journal of Political Economy* (Dec 1962).
J. JOHNSTON, *Statistical Cost Analysis* (New York: McGraw-Hill, 1960).
A. E. KAHN, 'Pricing Objectives in Large Companies. Comment', *American Economic Review* (Sep 1959).
N. KALDOR, 'Market Imperfections and Excess Capacity', *Economica*, no. 2 (1935).
D. R. KAMERSCHEN, 'The Influence of Ownership and Control on Profit Rates', *American Economic Review* (June 1968).
—, 'Testing the Sales Maximisation Hypothesis', *Rivista Internazionale di Scienze Economiche e Commerciali* (June 1968).
—, 'An Empirical Test of Oligopoly Theories', *Journal of Political Economy* (July 1968).
—, 'A Theory of Conglomerate Mergers. Comment', *Quarterly Journal of Economics* (Nov 1970).
M. KAMIEN and N. SCHWARTZ, 'Limit Pricing and Uncertain Entry' *Econometrica* (May 1971).

M. KAMIEN and N. SCHWARTZ, 'Uncertain Entry and Excess Capacity', *American Economic Review* (Dec. 1972).

A. D. KAPLAN, J. B. DIRLAM and R. F. LANZILLOTTI, *Pricing in Big Business: A Case Approach* (Washington D.C.: The Brookings Institution, 1958).

C. KAYSEN, 'Another View of Corporate Capitalism', *Quarterly Journal of Economics* (Feb 1965).

R. S. KOOT and D. A. WALKER, 'Short-run Cost Functions of a Multi-Product Firm', *Journal of Industrial Economics* (Apr 1971).

D. A. KUEHN, 'Stock Market Valuation and Acquisitions: An Empirical Test of One Component of Managerial Utility', *Journal of Industrial Economics* (Apr 1969).

D. KUEHN and R. MARRIS, 'New Light on Take-Overs', *The Banker* (July 1973).

R. E. KUENNE (ed.), *Monopolistic Competition Theory: Studies in Impact. Essays in Honour of Edward H. Chamberlin* (New York: Wiley, 1966).

R. F. LANZILLOTTI, 'Competitive Price Leadership – A Critique of Price Leadership Models', *Review of Economics and Statistics* (Feb 1957).

—, 'Pricing Objectives in Large Companies', *American Economic Review* (Dec 1958).

—, 'Pricing Objectives in Large Companies. Reply', *American Economic Review* (Sep 1959).

R. J. LARNER, 'Ownership and Control in the 200 Largest Non-Financial Corporations, 1929 and 1963', *American Economic Review* (Sep 1966).

—, *Management Control and the Large Corporation* (New York: Dunellen, 1970).

L. B. LAVE, 'An Empirical Approach to the Prisoner's Dilemma Game', *Quarterly Journal of Economics* (Aug 1962).

—, 'Factors Affecting Co-operation in the Prisoner's Dilemma', *Behavioural Science* (Jan 1965).

C. A. LEE, 'Organization Theory and Business Behaviour', in *Interdisciplinary Studies in Business Behaviour*, ed. J. W. McGuire (Cincinatti: South-Western, 1962).

H. LEIBENSTEIN, 'Allocative Efficiency versus X-Efficiency', *American Economic Review* (June 1966).

—, 'Organisational or Frictional Equilibria, X-Efficiency, and the Rate of Innovation', *Quarterly Journal of Economics* (Nov 1969).

—, 'Comment on the Nature of X-Efficiency', *Quarterly Journal of Economics* (May 1972).

—, 'Competition and X-Efficiency – Reply', *Journal of Political Economy* (May 1973).

R. A. LESTER, 'Marginalism, Minimum Wages, and Labour Markets', *American Economic Review* (1947).
H. H. LIEBHAFSKY, 'The Geometry of Kinky Oligopoly: Marginal Cost, The Gap, and Price Behaviour: Comment', *Southern Economic Journal* (July 1972).
R. G. LIPSEY, *An Introduction to Positive Economics*, 3rd edn (London: Weidenfeld & Nicolson, 1971).
W. G. LLEWELLEN, 'Management and Ownership in the Large Firm', *Journal of Finance* (May 1969).
B. J. LOASBY, 'Management Economics and the Theory of the Firm', *Journal of Industrial Relations* (1966–7).
—, 'Managerial Decision Processes', *Scottish Journal of Political Economy* (Nov 1967).
—, 'Hypothesis and Paradigm in the Theory of the Firm', *Economic Journal* (Dec 1971).
S. LOFTHOUSE, 'On Paradigms, Methodology and the Theory of the Firm', *Rivista Internazionale di Scienze Economiche e Commerciali* (Mar 1973 and June 1973).
D. E. LOGUE and P. A. NAERT, 'A Theory of Conglomerate Mergers. Comment and Extension', *Quarterly Journal of Economics* (Nov 1970).
R. E. LOW, *Modern Economic Organization* (Homewood, Ill.: Irwin, 1970).
R. D. LUCE and H. RAIFFA, *Games and Decisions* (New York: Wiley, 1957).
H. F. LYDALL, 'Conditions of New Entry and the Theory of Price', *Oxford Economic Papers* (1955) pp. 300–11.
B. D. MABRY, 'Sales Maximization vs. Profit Maximization: Are They Inconsistent?', *Western Economic Journal* (Mar 1968).
B. D. MABRY and D. SIDERS, 'An Empirical Test of the Sales Maximization Hypothesis', *Southern Economic Journal* (Jan 1967).
B. J. MCCORMACK *et al.*, *Introducing Economics* (Harmondsworth: Penguin, 1974).
R. MCGUCKIN, 'Entry, Concentration Change, and Stability of Market Shares', *Southern Economic Journal* (Jan 1972).
F. MACHLUP, 'Marginal Analysis and Empirical Research', *American Economic Review* (Sep 1946).
—, 'Rejoinder to an Anti-Marginalist', *American Economic Review* (Mar 1947).
—, *The Economics of Seller's Competition* (Baltimore: Johns Hopkins Press, 1952).
—, 'Theories of the Firm, Marginalist, Behavioural, Managerial', *American Economic Review* (Mar 1967).

F. MACHLUP, 'Corporate Management National Interests and Behavioural Theory', *Journal of Political Economy* (Oct 1967).

P. J. MCNULTY, 'A Note on the History of Perfect Competition', *Journal of Political Economy* (Aug 1967).

—, 'Economic Theory and the Meaning of Competition', *Quarterly Journal of Economics* (Nov 1968).

H. M. MANN, 'Seller Concentration, Barriers to Entry and Rates of Return in Thirty Industries, 1950–1960', *Review of Economics and Statistics* (Aug 1966).

—, 'A Note on Barriers to Entry and Long Run Profitability', *Antitrust Bulletin* (winter 1969).

—, 'The Interaction of Barriers and Concentration. A Reply', *Journal of Industrial Economics* (July 1971).

—, 'Concentration, Barriers to Entry, and Rates of Return Revisited. A Reply', *Journal of Industrial Economics* (Apr 1973).

H. MANNE, 'Mergers and the Market for Corporation Control', *Journal of Political Economy* (Apr 1965).

E. MANSFIELD, *The Economics of Technological Change* (New York: Norton, 1968).

J. MARGOLIS, 'The Analysis of the Firm, Rationalism, Conventionalism, and Behaviourism', *Journal of Business* (July 1958).

—, 'Traditional and Revisionist Theories of the Firm. A Comment', *Journal of Business* (Apr 1959).

J. MARKHAM, 'An Alternative Approach to the Concept of Workable Competition', *American Economic Review* (June 1950).

—, 'The Nature and Significance of Price Leadership', *American Economic Review* (Dec 1951).

R. MARRIS, 'A Model of the "Managerial" Enterprise', *Quarterly Journal of Economics* (May 1963).

—, *The Economic Theory of 'Managerial Capitalism'* (London: Macmillan, 1964).

—, 'The Modern Corporation and Economic Theory', in *The Corporate Economy*, ed. R. Marris and A. Wood (London: Macmillan, 1971) ch. 9.

—, 'Why Economics Needs a Theory of the Firm', *Economic Journal*, supplement (Mar 1972).

E. S. MASON (ed.), *The Corporation in Modern Society* (Harvard U.P., 1959).

R. T. MASSON, 'Executive Motivations, Earnings, and Consequent Equity Performance', *Journal of Political Economy* (Dec 1971).

P. MAUNDER, 'Price Leadership; An Appraisal of its Character in Some British Industries', *Business Economist* (autumn 1972).

G. C. MEANS, 'Industrial Prices and Their Relative Inflexibility', U.S. Senate, *Document B*, 74th Congress, 1st Session (Washington, D.C., 1935).

—, *Pricing, Power and the Public Interest* (New York: Harper & Row, 1962).

—, 'The Administered Price Thesis Reconfirmed', *American Economic Review* (June 1972).

K. MIDGLEY, 'How Much Control Do Shareholders Exercise?', *Lloyds Bank Review* (Oct 1974).

F. MODIGLIANI, 'New Developments on the Oligopoly Front', *Journal of Political Economy* (June 1958).

MONOPOLIES COMMISSION, *Parallel Pricing*, Cmnd. 5330 (London: H.M.S.O., July 1973).

R. J. MONSEN, 'Social Responsibility and the Corporation: Alternatives for the Future of Capitalism', *Journal of Economic Issues* (Mar 1972).

R. J. MONSEN, J. S. CHIU and D. E. COOLEY, 'The Effect of Separation of Ownership and Control on the Performance of the Large Firm', *Quarterly Journal of Economics* (Aug 1968).

R. J. MONSEN and A. DOWNS, 'A Theory of Large Managerial Firms', *Journal of Political Economy* (June 1965).

M. MOORE, 'Stigler on Inflexible Prices', *Canadian Journal of Economics* (Nov 1972).

D. C. MUELLER, 'The Firm Decision Process. An Econometric Investigation', *Quarterly Journal of Economics* (Feb 1967).

—, 'A Theory of Conglomerate Mergers', *Quarterly Journal of Economics* (Nov 1969).

—, 'A Theory of Conglomerate Mergers. Reply', *Quarterly Journal of Economics* (Nov 1970).

—, 'A Life Cycle Theory of the Firm', *Journal of Industrial Economics* (July 1972).

J. L. MURPHY, 'Effects of the Threat of Losses on Duopoly Bargaining', *Quarterly Journal of Economics* (May 1966).

T. A. MURPHY and Y-K. NG, 'Oligopolistic Interdependence and the Revenue Maximization Hypothesis – Note', *Journal of Industrial Economics* (Mar 1974).

NATIONAL BUREAU OF ECONOMIC RESEARCH, *Business Concentration and Price Policy* (Princeton U.P., 1955).

—, *Cost Behaviour and Price Policy* (New York: Kraus, 1963).

D. NEEDHAM, *Economic Analysis and Industrial Structure* (New York: Holt, Rinehart & Winston, 1972).

J. P. NETTL, 'A Note on Entrepreneurial Behaviour', *Review of Economic Studies* (Feb 1957).

F. D. NEWBURY, *A Businessman's Reaction to the Theory of Mono-*

polistic Competition, as quoted in W. W. Cooper, 'Theory of the Firm – Some Suggestions for Revision', *American Economic Review* (1949).

Y-K. Ng and R. Parish, 'Monopoly, X-Efficiency and the Measurement of Welfare Loss', *Economica* (Aug 1972).

G. W. Nutter, 'Duopoly, Oligopoly and Emerging Competition', *Southern Economic Journal* (Apr 1964).

D. Orr, 'The Determinants of Entry: A Study of the Canadian Manufacturing Industries', *Review of Economics and Statistics* (Feb 1974).

D. K. Osborne, 'The Role of Entry in Oligopoly Theory', *Journal of Political Economy* (Aug 1964).

—, 'The Duopoly Game; Output Variations', *American Economic Review* (1971).

—, 'On the Rationality of Limit Pricing', *Journal of Industrial Economics* (Sep 1973).

A. Oxenfeldt, 'Professor Markham on Price Leadership', *American Economic Review* (June 1952).

A. G. Papandreou, 'Some Basic Problems of the Theory of the Firm', in *A Survey of Contemporary Economics*, ed. B. Haley (Homewood, Ill.: Irwin, 1952).

W. Pardridge, 'Sales or Profit Maximization in Management Capitalism', *Western Economic Journal* (spring 1964).

P. Pashigian, 'Conscious Parallelism and the Kinky Oligopoly Demand Curve', *American Economic Review*, papers and proceedings (May 1967).

—, 'Limit Price and the Market Share of the Leading Firm', *Journal of Industrial Economics* (July 1968).

A. Patton, *Men, Money, and Motivation* (New York: International Publishers, 1961).

M. E. Paul, 'Notes on Excess Capacity', *Oxford Economic Papers* (1954) pp. 33–40.

I. F. Pearce, 'A Study in Price Policy', *Economica* (May 1956).

E. T. Penrose, 'Biological Analogies in the Theory of the Firm', *American Economic Review* (Dec 1952).

—, *The Theory of the Growth of the Firm* (Oxford: Blackwell, 1959).

V. Perlo, *The Empire of High Finance* (New York: International Publishers, 1957).

M. Peston, 'On the Sales Maximization Hypothesis', *Economica* (May 1959).

S. Peterson, 'Corporate Control and Capitalism', *Quarterly Journal of Economics* (Feb 1965).

E. S. Phelps (ed.), *Microeconomic Foundations of Employment and Inflation Theory* (London: Macmillan, 1970).

G. and P. POLANYI, 'Parallel Pricing: A Harmful Practice?', *Moorgate and Wall St Review* (spring 1974).

C. F. PRATTEN, *Economies of Scale in Manufacturing Industry*, University of Cambridge, Department of Applied Economics, Occasional Paper no. 28 (Cambridge U.P., 1971).

C. F. PRATTEN, R. M. DEAN and A. SILBERSTON, *The Economics of Large Scale Production in British Industry*, University of Cambridge, Department of Applied Economics. Occasional Paper no. 3 (Cambridge U.P., 1965).

W. J. PRIMEAUX Jr and M. R. BOMBALL, 'A Re-examination of the Kinky Oligopoly Demand Curve', *Journal of Political Economy* (July–Aug 1974).

G. PYATT, 'Profit Maximization and the Threat of New Entry', *Economic Journal* (June 1971).

H. K. RADICE, 'Control Type, Profitability and Growth in Large Firms', *Economic Journal* (Sep 1971).

A. RAPOPORT and C. ORWANT, 'Experimental Games: A Review', *Behavioural Science* (Jan 1962).

M. W. REDER, 'A Reconsideration of the Marginal Productivity Theory', *Journal of Political Economy* (1947).

S. A. RHOADES, 'Concentration, Barriers, and Rates of Return, A Note', *Journal of Industrial Economics* (Nov 1970).

—, 'Concentration, Barriers to Entry, and Rates of Return Revisited', *Journal of Industrial Economics* (Apr 1972).

G. B. RICHARDSON, 'Price Notification Schemes', *Oxford Economic Papers* (Nov 1967).

D. R. ROBERTS, *Executive Compensation* (New York: Glencoe, 1959).

J. ROBINSON, *The Economics of Imperfect Competition* (London: Macmillan, 1933).

H. B. ROSE and G. D. NEWBOULD, 'The 1967 Take-Over Boom', *Moorgate and Wall St Review* (autumn 1967).

R. ROSENBERG, 'Profit Constrained Revenue Maximization, Note', *American Economic Review* (Mar 1971).

K. W. ROTHSCHILD, 'Price Theory and Oligopoly', *Economic Journal* (Sep 1947).

C. K. ROWLEY (ed.), *Readings in Industrial Economics*, vols I and II (London: Macmillan, 1972).

—, *Steel and Public Policy* (New York: McGraw-Hill, 1971).

—, *Antitrust and Economic Efficiency* (London: Macmillan, 1973).

R. SANDMEYER, 'Baumol's Sales Maximization Model. Comment', *American Economic Review* (Dec 1964).

R. SANDMEYER and F. STEINDL, 'Conjectural Variation, Oligopoly, and Revenue Maximization', *Southern Economic Journal* (July 1970).

S. SANDMO, 'On the Theory of the Competitive Firm Under Price Uncertainty', *American Economic Review* (Mar 1971).

T. SAVING, 'Estimation of Optimum Plant Size by the Survivor Technique', *Quarterly Journal of Economics* (Nov 1961).

F. M. SCHERER, *Industrial Market Structure and Economic Performance* (Chicago: Rand McNally, 1970).

T. SCITOVSKY, 'A Note on Profit Maximization and its Implications', *Review of Economic Studies* (1943).

R. SHEEHAN, 'Proprietors in the World of Big Business', *Fortune* (15 June 1967).

J. P. SHELTON, 'Allocative Efficiency versus X-Efficiency. Comment', *American Economic Review* (Dec 1967).

W. G. SHEPHERD, 'On Sales Maximizing and Oligopoly Behaviour' *Economica* (Nov 1962).

—, 'What Does the Survivor Technique Show About Economies of Scale?', *Southern Economic Journal* (July 1967).

—, 'Entry as a Substitute for Regulation', *American Economic Review*, papers and proceedings (May 1973).

R. SHERMAN, *Oligopoly, An Empirical Approach* (Lexington, Mass.: D. C. Heath & Co., 1972).

R. SHERMAN and T. WILLETT, 'Potential Entrants Discourage Entry', *Journal of Political Economy* (Aug 1967).

M. SHUBIK, 'The Uses of Game Theory in Management Science', *Management Science* (1955).

—, *Strategy and Market Structure, Competition, Oligopoly and the Theory of Games* (New York: Wiley, 1959).

A. SILBERSTON, 'Surveys of Applied Economics: Price Behaviour of Firms', *Economic Journal* (Sep 1970).

—, 'Economies of Scale in Theory and Practice', *Economic Journal*, supplement (Mar 1972).

M. SILVER, 'Managerial Discretion and Profit Maximizing Behaviour. Some Further Comments', *Journal of Industrial Economics* (Apr 1967).

H. A. SIMON, 'A Behavioural Theory of Rational Choice', *Quarterly Journal of Economics* (Feb 1955).

—, 'Theories of Decision Making in Economics and Behavioural Science', *American Economic Review* (June 1959).

—, 'New Developments in the Theory of the Firm', *American Economic Review*, papers and proceedings (May 1962).

—, 'On the Concept of Organisational Goal', *Administrative Science Quarterly* (June 1964).

—, and C. BONINI, 'The Size Distribution of Business Firms', *American Economic Review* (Sep 1958).
J. SIMON, 'A Further Test of the Kinky Oligopoly Demand Curve', *American Economic Review* (Dec 1969).
A. SINGH, *Take-Overs* (Cambridge U.P., 1971).
J. SIZER, 'Note on the Determination of Selling Prices', *Journal of Industrial Economics* (Nov 1971).
R. C. SKINNER, 'The Determination of Selling Prices', *Journal of Industrial Economics* (July 1970).
D. S. SMITH and W. C. NEALE, 'The Geometry of Kinky Oligopoly: Marginal Cost, The Gap, and Price Behaviour', *Southern Economic Journal* (Jan 1971).
—, 'The Geometry of Kinky Oligopoly: Marginal Cost, The Gap, and Price Behaviour; Reply', *Southern Economic Journal* (July 1972).
E. P. SMITH, 'Interlocking Directorates Among the "Fortune 500"', *Antitrust Law and Economics Review* (summer 1970).
D. SMYTH, 'Sales Maximization and Managerial Effort. Note', *American Economic Review* (Sep 1969).
R. M. SOLOW, 'The Truth Further Refined. A Comment on Marris', *Public Interest* (spring 1968).
S. SOSNICK, 'A Critique of Concepts of Workable Competition', *Quarterly Journal of Economics* (Aug 1958).
P. SRAFFA, 'The Laws of Returns Under Competitive Conditions', *Economic Journal* (Dec 1926).
G. J. STIGLER, 'The Kinky Oligopoly Demand Curve and Rigid Prices', *Journal of Political Economy* (Oct 1947).
—, *Five Lectures on Economic Problems* (London: Longmans, Green, 1949).
—, 'Perfect Competition Historically Contemplated', *Journal of Political Economy* (Feb 1957).
—, 'The Economies of Scale', *Journal of Law and Economics* (Oct 1958).
—, 'Archibald *versus* Chicago', *Review of Economic Studies* (Feb 1963).
—, 'A Theory of Oligopoly', *Journal of Political Economy* (Feb 1964).
—, 'The Dominant Firm and the Inverted Umbrella', *Journal of Law and Economics* (Oct 1965).
—, *The Organization of Industry* (Homewood, Ill.: Irwin, 1968).
—, *The Theory of Price* (New York: Macmillan, 1966).
G. J. STIGLER and J. K. KINDAHL, *The Behaviour of Industrial Prices* (University of Columbia Press, 1970).
—, 'Industrial Prices as Administered by Dr. Means', *American Economic Review* (Sep 1973).

B. P. STIGUM, 'Entrepreneurial Choice Over Time Under Conditions of Uncertainty', *International Economic Review* (Oct 1969).

—, 'Competitive Equilibria Under Uncertainty', *Quarterly Journal of Economics* (Nov 1969).

P. STREETEN, 'Two Comments on the Articles by Mrs Paul and Professor Hicks', *Oxford Economic Papers* (Oct 1955).

P. M. SWEEZY, 'Demand Under Conditions of Oligopoly', *Journal of Political Economy* (Aug 1939).

P. SYLOS-LABINI, *Oligopoly and Technical Progress* (Harvard U.P., 1962).

F. W. TAUSSIG and W. S. BARKER, 'American Corporations and Their Executives', *Quarterly Journal of Economics* (Nov 1925).

L. G. TELSER, 'Monopolistic Competition: Any Impact Yet?', *Journal of Political Economy* (Mar 1968).

TEMPORARY NATIONAL ECONOMIC COMMITTEE (T.N.E.C.), *The Distribution of Ownership in the 100 Largest Non-Financial Corporations* monograph no. 29 (Washington, D.C.: AMS Press, 1940).

G. TINTNER, 'The Theory of Choice Under Subjective Risk and Uncertainty', *Econometrica* (1941).

R. TRIFFIN, *Monopolistic Competition and General Equilibrium Theory* (Harvard U.P., 1940).

G. TULLOCK, 'The New Theory of Corporations', in *Roads to Freedom*, ed. E. Streissler (London: Routledge & Kegan Paul, 1970).

M. A. UTTON, *Industrial Concentration* (Harmondsworth: Penguin, 1970).

D. VILLAREJO, 'Stock Ownership and the Control of Corporations', *New University Thought* (autumn 1961 and Feb 1962).

J. VON NEUMANN and O. MORGENSTERN, *Theory of Games and Economic Behaviour* (Princeton U.P., 1944).

H. VON STACKELBERG, *The Theory of the Market Economy*, trans. A. J. Peacock (London: W. Hodge & Co., 1952).

G. WALSHE, *Recent Trends in Monopoly in Great Britain* (Cambridge U.P., 1974).

A. A. WALTERS, 'Production and Cost Functions: An Econometric Survey', *Econometrica* (Jan–Apr 1963).

L. WAVERMAN, 'Sales Revenue Maximization – A Note', *Journal of Industrial Economics* (Nov 1968).

R. WEIL, 'A Systemmatic Look at the Prisoner's Dilemma', *Behavioural Science* (May 1966).

L. WEISS, 'The Survivor Technique and the Extent of Sub-optimal Capacity', *Journal of Political Economy* (June 1964).

J. WENDERS, 'Entry and Monopoly Pricing', *Journal of Political Economy* (Oct 1967).

—, 'Excess Capacity as a Barrier to Entry', *Journal of Industrial Economics* (Nov 1971).

J. F. WESTON, 'Pricing Behaviour of Large Firms', *Western Economic Journal*, vol. 10, no. 1 (1972).

J. R. WILDSMITH, *Managerial Theories of the Firm* (London: Martin Robertson, 1973).

P. WILES, *Price, Cost and Output* (Oxford: Blackwell, 1961).

J. H. WILLIAMSON, 'Profit, Growth and Sales Maximization', *Economica* (Feb 1966).

O. E. WILLIAMSON, 'Selling Expense as a Barrier to Entry', *Quarterly Journal of Economics* (Feb 1963).

—, 'A Model of Rational Managerial Behaviour', in *A Behavioural Theory of the Firm*, ed. R. M. Cyert and J. G. March (Englewood Cliffs, N.J., Prentice-Hall, 1963).

—, 'Managerial Discretion and Business Behaviour', *American Economic Review* (Dec 1963).

—, *The Economics of Discretionary Behaviour, Managerial Objectives in a Theory of the Firm* (Englewood Cliffs, N.J.: Prentice-Hall, 1964).

—, 'Economies as an Anti-trust Defence', *American Economic Review* (Mar 1968).

—, *Corporate Control and Business Behaviour* (Englewood Cliffs, N.J.: Prentice-Hall, 1970).

S. G. WINTER Jr, 'Economic "Natural Selection" and the Theory of the Firm', *Yale Economic Essays* (spring 1974).

A. WOOD, 'Economic Analysis of the Corporate Economy. A Survey and Critique', in *The Corporate Economy*, ed. R. Marris and A. Wood (London: Macmillan, 1971) ch. 2.

D. A. WORCESTER, 'Why Dominant Firms Decline', *Journal of Political Economy* (Aug 1957).

E. ZABEL, 'A Dynamic Model of the Competitive Firm', *International Economic Review* (June 1967).

—, 'The Competitive Firm and Price Expectations', *International Economic Review* (Oct 1969).

Index